Rental Property Investing

Learn to Create Wealth with Intelligent Buy and Hold Real Estate Investing

Mark De Luca

The content within this book has been derived from various sources. Please consult a licensed professional before attempting any techniques outlined in this book.

By reading this document, the reader agrees that under no circumstances is the author responsible for any losses, direct or indirect, that are incurred as a result of the use of the information contained within this document, including, but not limited to, errors, omissions, or inaccuracies.

Table of Contents

- Key #4- The Right Asset
- Key #5 - The Right Metrics

Types of Real Estate Properties

- Single Family
- Multifamily Properties
- Condos
- Real Estate Owner Properties (REOs)
- Rehabbers

Location Analysis

- Classes
    1. Grade A
    2. Grade B
    3. Grade C
    4. Grade D
- Crime areas

- Drug Use
- Schools
- Unemployment
- Population
- Transportation and Local Businesses
- Rental Yields
- Vacancy Rates
- Insurance and Taxes

- Two Simple Rules of Thumb
    1. The One Percent Rule
    2. The 70 Percent Rule
- Deal Sources
- MLS
- Direct Mail Campaigns
- Driving
- Evictions
- Craigslist

Introduction

Real-estate investing sounds like a great way to make money.

How often have you gone online and read about a 20-year-old kid who has a property "empire" worth millions? You might have picked up this book in the hopes of making a similar killing.

Well, sorry to burst your bubble, but that isn't happening anytime soon. If your idea of success is making millions by the end of the week or even within two years, rental property investing isn't the right method for you. Instead, investing in rentals will give you a steady and almost guaranteed path to wealth down the road. No one can tell you how long it's going to take, but there will be progress.

It takes a lot of work, but it's worth the investment of time and effort. Real estate has been one of the best ways to generate wealth in America over the past 100 years. The primary means of earning money in real estate has been through rental properties.

If you choose to not participate in this market, you're leaving a lot of money on the table. Perhaps the thought of assuming large amounts of debt scares you. Perhaps it's all the jargon and the ways in which seasoned real estate investors talk.

Whatever your issue is, I'm here to tell you that rental property investing isn't as complicated as it looks, though it isn't easy.

However, the things that you feel are complex are actually straightforward. It's the neglected stuff that creates problems. Anyone can learn some complicated-sounding lingo and throw it around. Very few can get their heads down and do the work needed to obtain success with their rental properties.

In this book, I'm going to walk you right from the very basics of rental property investing such as why they're a good option for investment, the methods to evaluate the numbers on a rental property, and how to scout great locations for a potential property. I'll also help you understand how you can evaluate the qualitative stuff. For example, how can you quickly figure out what an appropriate offer price is and how can you make sure the seller accepts it?

I'll also describe the mortgage approval process in complete detail. This is something many first time investors are intimidated by. Either they don't have the money or the sheer amount of paperwork is too much. Then, there's the problem of getting approved but finding out that the property you have your eye on is ineligible for financing!

People also have issues coming up with unexpected costs during the process. All of this will be addressed fully. By the time you're done reading with this book, you'll have a step by step plan of what you need to do in order to get approved and have as few surprises as possible.

Sounds great so far, doesn't it?

Problems

Rental property investing isn't as complex as it's made out to be. However, many people still fail at it. Why is this? The premise of rental investing isn't too hard to understand. Find a good property, find good tenants, and collect the rent. That's really all it boils down to. People still manage to mess it all up and find themselves dealing with a mountain of debt.

The answer can be found when you examine the mindsets of the landlords. Many people approach rental investing with a get rich

quick mindset and needless to say, this doesn't do them any favors. A get rich quick mindset only pushes them to chase after illusory gains. It also pushes them to assume large levels of debt in search of unrealistic gains.

The result is they end up depending on luck for success. This is in opposition to the methods that you'll learn in this book where you'll learn to rely on skill. While there is some luck involved, in the long run, your skill and a concrete plan will definitely create success for you.

Relying on luck isn't much of a plan. You might be successful once or twice in the short term, but chances are that you'll eventually end up back where you started or even worse.

Managing your leverage and debt levels in a deal is critical. It's also the one area where no one else can give you fixed templates to follow. Some people are very comfortable with assuming 90% leverage in their deals while some people feel safer with 70%. It comes down to your own risk profile and appetite.

Whatever your choice might be, rental property investing is a great way for you to increase your net worth. If this sounds like a good deal to you, then let's move forward and take a look at why rental properties are such a great investment choice.

Chapter 1 Why Rental Properties

Everyone I come into contact with knows that I love rental properties. I don't hide my appreciation for them in any way. By

the end of this book, neither will you. When people think of rental properties, the first things that often pop into their heads are troublesome tenants, phone calls at three in the morning, and other inconveniences.

It's true that some landlords are unfortunate enough to have to deal with this kind of stuff. I dealt with it when I first began as well. However, there's no denying that all of this can be avoided if you know what you're doing. If you take the wrong steps, you're going to end up with these kinds of problems. Luckily for you, I've committed pretty much every mistake in the book and you can now avoid them!

Rental properties are amazing because of the large number of benefits they provide. For starters, you don't need to have as much money as you think you need. By paying a sum of $10,000 you can control a property that's worth $300,000 through the power of financing. Don't take this as a recommendation to use high levels of leverage.

My objective with this example is to just show you how powerful it can be.

I'll walk you through the ins and outs of financing such properties later in this book. For now, simply understand that while you do need money to control properties, you don't need as much as you think you need to get started. The other great thing about rental property investing is that there isn't one single way to do it correctly.

If you're partial to one particular method of making money, then go ahead and implement that strategy. It isn't like the stock market where most strategies fail and in order to succeed you need to implement a few tried and tested ones. What if they don't suit you? There are no such fears when it comes to rental investing. Use the skills you have and execute your plan however you want. As long as you're following some simple principles, you'll be just fine.

With a rental property, you're in full control of your investment. you're not beholden to the stock market gods or any other outside forces. You will be dependent on the local real estate economy to a large extent, but even this isn't as exaggerated as it looks. You can choose your tenants wisely and choose to carry out maintenance on time on your property.

If you want to boost its value, there are ways you can do this easily. Unlike investing in a stock, you're not relying on a company's management or on their benevolence to pay you a dividend. You're the boss and you control everything. The best thing is there's always a demand for rental real estate. I mean, people need places to live, don't they?

As long as you take care of a few basic things, demand will always be present. In fact, the primary task you face is to choose which portion of the demand you wish to capture. There are different kinds of demand and you can tailor your strategies to suit any one of them. Very few other investment choices give you this much freedom.

As we move forward in time, more people are drowning in debt. This means their chances of getting approved for a mortgage are low. You, as a rental property owner, are in a prime position to capture and serve this demand. Rental property investing as a strategy isn't unique or revolutionary.

It's been used for ages now and it's straightforward. That is to say, it's unlikely that the mechanics of rentals are going to change. If someone wants to lease a property to live in it, they pay the landlord a sum of money every month.

This is standard practice everywhere in the world and it isn't tough to figure out.

While demand is pretty stable, the market itself is also quite stable. The fact is that the real estate market is nowhere near as unstable as the stock market is. It experienced a huge crash in 2007, but this was over a century in the making. Real estate is far less volatile than stocks and you can rest assured that as long as you're playing for the long term, you'll be fine.

There are many different kinds of rental properties you can purchase and this is yet another advantage that this investment method offers. You can buy small homes, large ones, multiple units, single units, duplexes, entire apartment buildings, and so on. In fact, no two properties are ever exactly the same even within these categories. There's always something new to learn and explore which keeps your enthusiasm up.

Rental property investing isn't easy to execute, but the steps are simple. There aren't too many things to watch out for once you get past the basics. Running the numbers is also very easy such that once you get used to it, you'll be doing them in your head without any issues.

This makes it easy to decide on whether to accept or pass on deals. There are no long lists of extraneous factors to consider. Another advantage is that real estate investing has a substantial support network. There are many investors, online support networks, and professionals involved in the industry.

If you've invested in the stock market previously, you'll know that insider trading is illegal. You cannot act on information that you receive before the public does. In real estate there's nothing like this to hold you back.

If you receive a tip on some neighborhood development coming up, you can jump in and buy all properties before their prices increase.

Finding bargains in real estate is a lot easier because the market isn't as saturated as the one for stocks is. Very few people are willing to put in the work to find great deals. As a result, you're more likely to find below market price deals. The extensive network of professionals operating in the field also makes it easy for you to source great deals.

Rental investing also makes it easy for you to earn passive income. This is income that you earn while you sleep. your tenant pays you rent every month and while you do need to carry out a few tasks related to maintenance, you don't need to be physically present every single moment in order to generate income. Your income is not dependent on your time anymore and this increases your potential to earn more money.

How do rental properties generate income for you? Let's take a deeper look.

Wealth Creators

There are four ways in which rental properties can build profits. Understand that some of these apply to real estate in general while some apply specifically to rental properties. Taking advantage of all four methods of wealth creation is necessary if you want to get rich in the process.

Price Appreciation

How much is a property worth today and how much was it worth 20 years ago? Chances are, it sold for a lot less 20 years back. This is an example of price appreciation. Real estate is a necessary good and, as a result, prices increase over time in line with inflation.

Also, land is scarce by nature. While the properties built on it can be replaced, this scarcity seeps into the value of the property as well. This means scarcity creates price appreciation over time. As populations increase, demand increases, but supply increases at a fixed rate. This means prices will increase.

The increase in the price of an asset over time creates what are called capital gains. Capital gains are great, but there's a dark side to them. It is possible for the market to become overheated and for prices to get disconnected from reality. This is what happened in the lead up to the recession in 2007.

Property investors noticed that no matter what they did, prices kept increasing and this caused them to neglect the math behind their deals. After all, if they could sell it to someone else for double the value a year from now, what did it matter that they were losing cash on a monthly basis on the property?

This sort of "greater fool" thinking led to a large number of poor decisions being made, and when the day of reckoning came, many were caught with their pants down. While capital gains are great, be careful of relying on them solely as you can only realize them as cash when you sell your asset.

You cannot use the price appreciation in the interim to pay your bills or to provide you with cash flow. Thus, relying on capital gains isn't very smart.

They can be substantial, but you want it to be backed up by something else (which is what the other three factors are.)

Capital gains can be created by investing cash into a property. For example, the strategy of flipping homes is an example where an investor forces capital appreciation by sprucing up the property. Note that in this strategy, the investor relies solely on capital gains and not on anything else. This is not what rental investing is all about.

Cash Flow

Cash flow ought to be redefined as being free cash flow. Every person in the field of business understands the value of this metric.

In business terms, free cash flow is what is left over after all of your expenses, other maintenance, and reinvestment needs have been met.

Let's say you're running a lemonade stand. Your expenses include the cost of lemons, sugar, water, cups and your stand. These are cash outflows. Your cash in flow is in the form of money earned by selling lemonade. The difference between the two is your free cash flow. Obviously, you want your inflows to be greater than outflows.

For simple businesses, free cash flow is the same as their earnings. With rental properties, it isn't as straightforward since you have non cash expenses like depreciation to account for. Therefore, earnings and free cash flow diverge. However, free cash flow is still far more important than earnings because it represents real hard cash that you can use to either pay bills or invest.

A rental property generates cash and you can use this to pay for its maintenance. You can also use this cash flow to pay for the mortgage of the property. Therefore, by buying a good rental property, you get paid to own it. In some cases, it's worth it to accept a small cash flow deficit but almost every great rental property deal will pay you cash to own an asset.

It's a bit like being paid to own a stock. This never happens in the stock market but in the rental property market, it's a reality.

Tax Credits

Taxes are ever present in any financial investment. You cannot avoid them. However, the American government gives you a ton of options to reduce them. The government recognizes the need that real estate investors fill in the economy. They're the ones that provide much needed housing facilities for those looking to rent places to live.

When tax time comes, you therefore get to keep a much larger portion of your income than the average American does. This boosts your rate of return and puts cash right back in your pocket. This doesn't mean you should invest in real estate just to save on taxes. However, it does offer these advantages that aren't available to other investors.

Free Asset Ownership

I briefly mentioned this before but it's necessary for you to understand just how powerful this is in terms of building wealth. When you finance a property, you're agreeing to pay a lender a certain amount of interest and a certain amount of the borrowed principal back to them over time.

Let's say you draw a mortgage with a bank and they ask you to pay $500 per month for the next 30 years. This $500 payment is divided between interest and principal payments. The principal represents the actual amount of money you borrowed and the interest represents the profit that the lender makes by loaning you the money.

In the beginning, $400 might be paid towards interest and $100 might go towards principal. As time goes on, this dynamic shifts and a larger portion of your payment pays down your principal. In real estate financing, this is called the amortization schedule. It tells you what the proportion is between interest and principal payments. The faster you pay down the principal, the quicker you pay off your loan.

Interest represents money you haven't borrowed but you need to pay for the privilege of borrowing it. It is a cost of ownership for you. If you paid all cash upfront for a property, this isn't an issue. However, most people don't have that much cash lying around to buy a $200,000 property in full.

If you decide to live in the house that you mortgaged, then you've opened yourself up to capital gains down the road but in the short term, you've created a $500 cash outflow for yourself. This places additional burden on your cash flow and makes it even more important for you to ensure you don't lose your job or source of income.

Now imagine if you rented the property out and got paid $500 every month by your tenants. Your capital gains exposure is intact but you've now created a cash inflow that balances the outflow. As a result, your finances aren't stretched. You get to keep the asset for free in terms of cash flow since you're not paying anything extra to acquire it.

This is why rental property investing is so powerful. Your asset pays you to own it. There are very few other opportunities that allow this level of convenience in terms of ownership.

Money Required

All of this is great, you might be thinking, but how much money is needed to take part in real estate? Let's get the simple math out of the way first. In order to invest in any property you need to have, realistically, at least 20% of its value saved up. It depends on the financing route you decide to pursue.

Conventional lenders will require you to pay at least 23% of the property upfront with 20% functioning as a down payment and the remaining amount accounting for closing costs. I'll explain these in more detail in the chapter on financing. If you decide to go down the Federal Housing Authority (FHA) route then you could put down as little as six percent of the property's price.

For safety's sake it's best to save at least 20% of the total price of the property. This will give you a lot of flexibility in determining what kind of a property you can go after and how much you want your monthly payment to be. The more money you pay upfront, the lower is the loan you'll need to seek and the lower your monthly payment will be.

This means you will realistically need to save five figures before you can consider getting started in real estate. This is a good thing since you'll have more time to do your homework! Something that is important to understand is that the money you pay upfront is very different from the risk inherent in your investment.

The risk present in any investment is the probability that you will lose money. A person can pay $30,000 down to finance a $100,000 property (this drawing a $70,000 mortgage) while another could pay zero down and secure a $70,000 mortgage. In both cases, the loan sought is exactly the same. So who's at greater risk?

It's impossible to tell with just this information because we don't know the specifics of their deals. The zero down investor could have close to no risk because they've bought a great property that will generate lots of cash flow for them, to the tune of $1,000 per month.

The 30% down investor might be paying just $400 per month in mortgage payments but their rental income might be just $200.

This means despite paying more money down and owning more of the property (30% of it), this investor is at greater risk because they've created a cash outflow for themselves. What if the market value of the properties drops to $50,000 each?

In this scenario, if the zero down investor has enough cash flow to continue to pay their mortgage, they can ride the tough market out. However, the 30% down investor's cash flow burden still exists. If they happen to lose their job, they'll face foreclosure. They cannot even sell their property since they'll receive just $50,000 for it. They'll owe $70,000 to the bank!

This situation occurred in 2007 and it's called being "underwater" on your mortgage. If you owe more on your property than what you can sell it for, you're underwater. As you can see, from this example it looks like the 30% down investor overreached and invested in a poor property. The zero down investor did proper research and managed to ride the storm despite not putting any money down.

I'm not saying zero money down loans are a good idea by any means. These often come with many caveats that most beginners fail to account for. Hence my advice to save at least 20% of the property you have your eye on.

The purpose of this example was to show you that risk isn't about money. It's about the possibility that you might lose your money. It's important for you to prepare for risk and to account for the ways in which risk could present itself. This is why smart rental investors always save up to six month's worth of expenses as cash in the bank.

This way, if the property happens to be vacant or if tenants are not found, there is adequate backup to ensure they don't run into trouble.

Difficulties

Not everything is a bed of roses and prudent investors understand the risks and difficulties before jumping in. Here are some of the most difficult things about rental investing from my perspective.

Time

Wealth building in rental real estate investing is a function of repeated action taken over a long period of time. It is possible to make millions, but you cannot expect them to manifest overnight. You need to be prepared for the long haul. There will be moments when you'll feel as if you're making no progress at all. You'll have to deal with headaches and you'll have a few nightmarish tenants to deal with.

The successful investor is the one who stays calm throughout all of these times and doesn't panic or try to switch gears. You need to trust the process and keep executing your plan. As simple as this sounds, many people don't do it. They fall for get rich quick schemes and chase the hottest new strategy.

In real estate, there are no new strategies. The laws have been the same for a long time now as have the strategies. Even fancy sounding ones such as "house hacking" have been used for ages. So, stay strong and stay the course.

Time Consuming

There are two ways of looking at this. The first is to adopt a pessimistic mindset and think you need to do everything. The second is to act like a business owner and outsource tasks and develop processes. Make no mistake, if you don't do this, owning a rental property will become a full time job. That's precisely what you want to avoid.

If mismanaged, your rental property will become a nightmare. You'll need to deal with issues cropping up all of a sudden and you'll have no control over your time. A pipe might burst when you're on vacation and you'll be responsible to fix it no matter what your current situation is.

Successful landlords create a support network that handles all of these tasks for them. They work with the right professionals who are efficient. Of course, such help doesn't come cheap but it's worth it in the long run. It's important for you to treat your rentals as a business. If you don't, you'll find that your rental will end up running your life.

There's a positive side to all of this. Once you have two or three rentals bringing in around $3,000 per month, it'll be hard for you to stop talking about the cash you're flush with. You'll likely spend nights wondering what some property might rent for or how much you can invest into a property you have your eye on.

Success is addictive and once you begin to experience it, you'll want more of it. This is a good thing, but it can be dangerous if you are not careful and ignore internal responsibilities in business and in life.

Dealing With People

This is the most difficult part of being a rental investor and, frankly, it's one that will drive you crazy. The nature of real estate investing is such that you'll need to work with other people. The first person you'll have to deal with will be your banker or loan officer. This eagle eyed professional might do their best to keep money away from you and will propose absurd terms no investor would ever agree to. At times it'll seem as if they're blind and lack common sense.

Then, there are contractors. Some of them won't show up, the ones who do show up will do a shoddy job and will charge you double for the privilege. You'll ask them to paint the walls white and they'll paint them purple. Then, there are the tenants. You'll

encounter some truly hall of fame worthy tenants if you're an investor for a long enough period of time.

There will be the deadbeats who don't pay on time and are always diving from one crisis into another. There will be pet lovers who decide to groom snakes despite your property being pet unfriendly. There might even be drug users.

There will be people who will need to be evicted and leave a royal mess behind.

All of this will test your patience to the extreme. It's easy to lose hope in humanity when you're a rental property investor! A lot of these problems can be managed through intelligent screening but, every once in a while, someone will slip through. If you find it particularly difficult to deal with people and wish to remain anonymous, then rental property investing isn't for you. There are other ways of making money in both real estate and the stock market.

Paperwork

Want to be a rental investor? Be prepared to organize more paper than you've ever seen in your life! From payment receipts to leases to contractor bills to tax lien receipts you'll need to keep track of them all. You'll have to keep your books using QuickBooks or some other software and these have a learning curve of their own.

You'll have to deal with receiving pieces of paper in the mail everyday that will demand your attention. They will need to be sorted, filed and logged. You'll need to have proof for everything. Then, there's the monstrosity known as tax time. If you own more than one property, taxes take a life of their own.

If you aren't the most organized person then you either hire someone else to do all this for you or you learn the skills you need. Fast. Do not get into rental investing unless you're prepared to deal with the rigors of a regular filing system. Currently, most investors store everything on their computers and have backups for all data.

Risk of Loss

This is the biggest difficulty you need to understand. At the end of the day, you're making an investment. Every investment carries a risk of loss.

Once you become well versed with rental property investing you'll notice that the majority of great deals you'll find will come from real estate owned (REO) properties. These are foreclosures that are being offered to other buyers.

The sellers were probably real estate investors who could not make their investment work for them. Why do so many investors fail? If real estate investing is straightforward, then why are there so many foreclosures in the country? My personal guess is that people's mindsets are not wired for business. They run things improperly and don't take the time to understand the difficulties and risks involved.

This is why I'm taking the time to list all of the negatives you'll have to deal with. The positives are huge and ample but if you can't handle the negatives or learn to live with them, you're not going to enjoy the process. This will most likely lead you to failure.

As you read this book, take a lot of time to understand the risks as well as the logic behind the methods I'm going to show you.

Above all else, make sure you maintain the right mindset for success.

As long as you avoid doing the wrong things, there are just a few things you'll need to get right. Tick those boxes and you'll see your wealth multiply exponentially.

Chapter 2

Keys to Rental Investing Success

I must warn you, I'm going to go all "self help coach" on you in this chapter. I believe it is essential for you to possess the right mindset

if you wish to be successful. The fact is that the numbers say the odds are against you when it comes to rental investing success. I believe this is purely because people simply haven't received the right mental guidance to make rental investing work.

They've been promised the wrong things and have been given an incomplete picture of what it takes to succeed. As I've mentioned before, it's simple to succeed at investing in rental properties. The reason most people fail is because they equate simple with easy. They adopt a lazy approach to their business without even knowing it.

It's important that you make sure your head is in the right place before you begin your journey. This chapter is going to give you five keys that will ensure you're successful. You'll still need to do the work. However, by having these five things in place you'll ensure that you're working smart and that your efforts will pay dividends.

Key #1 - The Right Thoughts

Ludwig van Beethoven, the famous classical music composer, was deaf towards the end of his illustrious career. The man composed some of the greatest foundational works of music ever created by hearing the music in his head and putting it onto paper. He must have been an immense prodigy, right? He was probably the wunderkind of whichever music school he attended.

Wrong. When he was a child, Beethoven's teachers recommended he try something else in life because he couldn't compose a note to save his life. There are stories of born geniuses, but Beethoven wasn't one. Neither was Thomas Edison. Babe Ruth was once given the title "The Strikeout King" as well.

Colonel Sanders was an unsuccessful hustler [and one time midwife] until the age of 65 when he got tired of people having gunfights at his gas station and decided to fry some chicken instead.

There are far more people who have had to work for their success after being told they were no good than ones who were born into it (Dweck, 2016). This isn't a pep talk, it's a fact.

According to Stanford University professor Carol Dweck, the most important determiner of success is your mindset.

More specifically, you're more likely to succeed if you have a growth mindset as opposed to a fixed mindset.

A growth mindset believes that everything can be learned with enough work. You don't know enough about rental property investing right now. When you go online and hear Grant Cardone talk about his $350 million real estate holdings, you might think you'll never reach that stage.

These are indicators of a fixed mindset. This mindset believes you're born with your talents and that's all you'll ever have. This is neither true nor productive. All of us learn how to talk, walk and behave. As kids, we revelled in exasperating the adults around us with our constant refrain of "why?" We didn't mind falling flat on our faces and getting back up with a grin.

Somewhere along the way we forgot this fact and began taking things far too seriously. You cannot take your rental properties, whether successful or a failure, with you beyond your grave. Let those pressures go and treat it as a game instead.

This means, every game has its rules and in order to win you need to learn them and then understand which ones to break. Have you ever seen a successful professional athlete?

All of them do something that breaks the mold. It could be Tiger Woods changing his swing, Michael Jordan being, well, Jordan, and Tom Brady changing the way athletes think about nutrition and preparation.

All of these athletes learned the rules of their craft and polished themselves to a high degree before they started exerting their natural creativity. Your task is the same. The good news is you don't need to become the quarterbacking G.O.A.T to achieve success. All you need to do is follow simple principles and learn when you can push their boundaries a bit.

Doing this at first is not a wise choice. After all, when you begin investing, you need to learn the associated principles. However, as long as you have the belief that you can do anything you put your mind to, you'll keep learning and your knowledge will compound. One fine day, you'll realize that you're able to evaluate rental properties in a few seconds without having to even look at the place physically.

What do You Want?

If you were to ask most people whether they want a million dollars, almost everyone would say yes. The only ones who'd say no are those who have more than that amount of cash in the bank.

Ask yourself this question right now. Do you want a million dollars in cash? Notice the thoughts that come into your head. Write them down if need be.

Now, examine the thoughts that sprung up. Did they have to do with spending the million? Did you think you'd buy all the rental properties you can lay your hands on? Did you see yourself buying fancy clothes, a new home, car and so on?

If you did, you're not alone.

The fact is, most people want the pleasure of spending a million dollars. They don't want to envision putting in the work it takes to make that amount of cash. They don't want to think about the time it takes to master certain skills and then put it into action. Once you make the switch from wanting to spend to wanting to learn and practice skills, that's when you'll become successful.

There's no shortcut to success at anything. You need to follow through consistently and do the work. It's perfectly fine to envision enjoying the fruits of your labor, but you cannot make that your only goal. You need to use that picture to fuel you to do the work right now. So take a mental inventory of yourself and be the person that loves doing the work.

Don't take yourself too seriously while you're at it. Treat it as a game and you'll have fun even if you make a fool of yourself. This is going to happen at some point no matter how much you try to avoid it so you might as well enjoy it.

Key #2 - The Right Sources

So, you're all ready to play the game, and now need to learn the rules. Where do you start? There are so many websites and sources of information, all of it can be overwhelming at first. The logical place to start is with books [like this one]. There are many books on real estate investing and those are the best ways to begin learning the foundational strategies.

Once you're done reading this book, here are some other ones that will help you along your journey:

1.   Long-Distance Real Estate Investing by David Greene

2.   The Book on Rental Property Investing by Brandon Turner

3.   Trump: The Art of the Deal by Donald Trump and Tony Schwartz

4.   The Millionaire Real Estate Investor by Gary Keller

5.   The Book on Investing in Real Estate with No (and Low) Money Down by Brandon Turner

6.   How to be a Real Estate Investor by Phil Pustejovsky

Read these and you'll find many more books that will suggest themselves to you. All of these books present a slightly different take on real estate investment success. Another great source of education is YouTube. Start following channels that cover real estate investing.

It's also a good idea to join a forum such as the one on Bigger Pockets and start asking your questions there. This will help you network with people who are more knowledgeable than you and those who are on the same level as you are. When the time comes you'll be able to find yourself an accountability buddy or even a business partner.

Podcasts are a great resource to tap into if you want to educate yourself. Load them up beforehand and listen to them while you drive to work. There are many great ones to listen to including ones hosted by Grant Cardone, Brandon Turner and Mike Simmons. Simmons' show titled Just Start Real Estate is particularly helpful for beginners. Another good one is The Real Estate Guys Radio Show.

You might be overwhelmed and won't understand everything these people are talking about at first. That's okay. You're still learning. In fact, you're always learning. Keep gaining exposure to the real estate world and you'll slowly but surely manage to train your brain to think like these people.

As Jim Rohn once said, you are the sum of the five people you associate with the most. Note that associate doesn't always mean "hang out." In the beginning, you won't have a circle of friends and associates who are in the real estate world. This is fine. You can associate with the people you want to be like by listening to what they say on YouTube and through podcasts.

This is how you can train your mind to believe that you can achieve their levels of success. Be wary of people who sell you this feature for a price though. There are many gurus who sell real estate investment courses for a price. Some of them are very good as well. However, the information that is contained in these courses are often freely available. The only reason people sign up to these courses is because they feel they need someone to push them to take action.

If this applies to you, understand that only you can motivate yourself. If you don't start with the right "why" you'll never push yourself to do the work. If you still struggle for motivation, get an accountability partner who can ask you how you're progressing towards your goals.

By monitoring their progress as well, you're more likely to hold yourself accountable.

After all, you can't hold someone else accountable without making sure you're doing your partner.

Key #3 - The Right Plan

Let me say this right now. The right plan that I'm talking about here is not your business plan. This plan is going to document your "why".

Why do you want to invest in real estate? What's the end goal here? Do you want to create enough passive income so as to not have to depend on a job anymore?

Do you want to travel the world and not have to worry about money? Do you want to spend more time with your family and kids? Everyone has different goals and your plan begins with defining your "why." This is what will motivate you when times get tough. It's best to write this out on a piece of paper and read it every day, when you wake up and before you go to bed.

Understand that your plan can change. The plans you had when you were 16, for example, have probably changed today. Start with your why and then develop a roadmap.

Where do you want to be by the end of the year? How about a year from now? Five years? 10 years? 20 years?

You'll find that when developing these goals, you won't know how to get there. This is a good thing. The "how" isn't important. This goes back to the first key you learned about. As long as you believe that you can learn your way forward, you'll get anywhere you want to be.

You will have some idea to get to your year-end goal or the goal that's one year away from today. Write these out. They don't need to be super accurate or even practical. The thing that most people get wrong about goal setting is they get caught up in the how. This keeps changing as you gain knowledge, and as a result, most people think they're being indecisive. If anything, the opposite is true.

By adapting to new knowledge you're actually executing your plan. The worst thing you can do is give up because you think your goals keep changing. They will change. The only thing that remains constant is your "why". The specifics of this might change as well but that's okay. After all, if you formed a goal to buy a fancy toy for yourself when you were five years old, it's unrealistic to expect this to remain in place for the rest of your life.

This process is meant to jog your mind and to get it to associate it with your goals.

Eventually, you'll begin to see real estate investing as being a viable method of generating the income and goals you want.

You'll begin to apply your natural creativity to your deals and will start seeing opportunities everywhere.

Have you ever wanted to buy something and then realized that you're now seeing that thing everywhere? Why is this? It's because your mind is focused on that object and is searching for opportunities. This process will get it focused on your goals and on the method to get there. This is how you'll open new paths for yourself.

Key #4- The Right Asset

The asset in question is real estate properties. However, not every property is the right asset for you and your plan. You'll learn more about investing strategies as you read this book so keep this point in mind. A property that makes for a great house hack might not be the best solution.

A multi-family property might work very well for one strategy but it might create a burden when implementing another. The key to investing success is to understand what assets and liabilities are. An asset is something that reduces your financial burden and makes you wealthy over time. A liability is something that increases your burden and creates more problems for you.

For example, drawing a mortgage and living in your own home is a huge liability. You're increasing your monthly cash outflow in exchange for a future capital gain that may or may not come.

With real estate it's more probable that it will come but you can't be certain of this. Think of all the people who waited for 30 years to cash in their capital gains and then ran into the market of 2007. Some parts of the country haven't recovered as yet from that crash.

This has nothing to do with the property itself. It could be an excellent place. However, is it the sort of property that it makes sense for you to rely on capital gains? Would it have been a better-turned rental?

Ask yourself these questions when evaluating properties.

If you don't ask these questions, you'll end up turning an asset into a liability. Many people do this inadvertently with the method I just described. This is also why many investors go broke investing in rental properties. They don't define their plans well enough and take the advice to treat it as a "game" to mean they shouldn't be serious about it.

That's not what the advice means. You need to play the game according to the right rules and keep learning. Think of how children learn and the attitude they take to questioning and learning through experience. That's what you need to do as well. Don't assume that any one is going to do the trick for you because you can go broke investing in the wrong properties.

Key #5 - The Right Metrics

A metric is a standard that is used to measure something. When it comes to real estate investing, you're going to have to track a bunch of metrics. Don't worry, though, this isn't as troublesome as you might think it is. However, it does require you to put in a lot of work.

Many property owners get complacent or, even worse, start tracking the wrong metrics in an attempt to convince themselves that everything's fine. Much like the meme where a dog is sitting inside a house on fire, they tell themselves "everything's fine" and end up losing their shirt.

Metrics are tricky because they can be designed in ways to present the picture you want to see. For example, many property owners notice the declining cash flow of their properties and choose to ignore it by looking at the capital appreciation instead. They could also do it the other way around. Increasing cash flow is not sustainable if the value of the property is falling.

This is because there are broader economic movements happening that are going to affect the ability of your tenants to pay you on time.

You can massage yourself with the high rental yield all day, but unless you are honest with yourself and view property metrics realistically, you're not going to be successful.

Being a good real estate investor, or a business person of any kind, means you need to be willing to face facts. We put a lot of ourselves into our properties and it can be painful to face the fact that our investments aren't working out. The best thing to do is to figure out how to extricate ourselves from this situation instead of convincing ourselves that everything is fine.

The best metrics to look at when it comes to real estate is cash flow and property values. There are a few ratios that evaluate the performance of your property in this regard and it's best to keep track of them. Keep in mind that the great thing about real estate is you can force appreciation to a certain extent. Ensuring better cash flow can often be as simple as giving your property a new lick of paint or installing better lights within it.

There are numerous ways to get creative with generating additional cash flow from your investment so keep your eyes open for these factors. Above all else, you need to adopt a business person's mindset. Your properties exist to make you money. Your tenants are your customers. This means you need to provide them with great service, but you also need to be firm about the money they pay you for that service.

Don't get emotionally attached to your property. Some investors get attached to their first property and are unwilling to let it go even when the metrics tell them it's time to do so. This is not the correct way to invest. Get attached to the money the property is bringing you instead of getting attached to the property itself.

Always choose sensible metrics to evaluate performance. This is both before and after making the investment. Managing an investment is a balancing act. You'll need honest feedback about how well you're doing and the right metrics do this. Recognize them for what they are and follow what they're telling you.

Chapter 3 Types of Real Estate Properties

You want to invest in rental real estate and have already mapped out a plan to begin saving up some money. The question is what kinds of properties you want to invest in? There are many different types of properties out there and in order to be successful

you need to know the pros and cons of each.

Each property type has its own cons attached to it. You can't have the positive without the negatives and if more real estate investors realized this there wouldn't be as many failures.

Single Family

This is your typical house that you think of when anyone mentions a property. It's mostly located in the suburbs and as the name suggests, it is used by families who need more space. Typically, these will contain one kitchen, bathrooms, bedrooms and will be constructed on their own plot of land.

Owning this home is, by definition, the American Dream and is therefore the most common type of property that exists. The good thing about single family residences is that they have a robust market backing them up.

Most real estate agents deal in these kinds of properties and the majority of demand centers around these kinds of homes.

Banks and lenders are also well versed with financing these homes and it's easier to score financing for such properties. There are many single family residences out there and more are being built everyday around the country. The abundance of these homes is only dwarfed by the demand for them and as a result, exit strategies are pretty easy to put into action.

This is because you'll always have a willing buyer for these homes. Slight improvements to such properties usually result in a large boost in value thanks to this type of demand. The great thing about owning a single-family residence is that, traditionally,

The tenant is responsible for paying all utility bills. This leaves you liable for just the insurance and the taxes.

The mortgage and repairs are on your plate as well, but you are the property owner so it makes sense these would fall on your shoulders. The fact that a single family typically lives in such properties makes them easier to manage. Typically, these homes will be rented by young families who are expecting a kid or two in the coming years.

Such tenants tend to stay for a while in one place which leaves you without any headaches in terms of finding replacement tenants.

Such tenants also tend to be more stable since they'll need to hold a regular job or have a strong source of income to be able to fund their lifestyle. You'll also have to deal with less hassles since these kinds of neighborhoods tend to be quiet and safe. If any troubles do occur, your tenant will most likely call the cops and not you at ungodly hours of the day.

The best part of single family residences is that, thanks to their pent up demand, their appreciation is almost guaranteed. This means capital appreciation is built into the value of the property. This doesn't mean they're expensive though. While the cost per unit of a single family residence is high, the overall cost tends to be lower than a multifamily property or a commercial property.

Add to this fact that they're easier to finance and it's easy to see their mass appeal amongst investors.

Disadvantages

The high cost per unit of a single family residence might not always be justified. For example, if you find a single family residence for $100,000 and a duplex for $150,000 your cost per unit is

$100,000 and $75,000 respectively. Two units of the duplex can produce two separate streams of cash for you and give you more stability.

While the overall price of a single family is low, it makes sense to sometimes absorb a higher mortgage to generate better cash returns

on your investment. Single family homes produce stability but this doesn't mean they're always the better investment. For one thing, they're slower to scale.

Scaling, in this case, means your ability to build your wealth from one property and move those gains to finance the next one. If you buy one property at a time, it's going to take you a lot longer to build up to a level where you have 100 properties. Multi-unit properties have better appreciation potential since you could improve all of them individually. The overall price rise after such improvements will be larger than the sum of their parts.

Another reason it's hard to scale with single family residences is that you will run into the loan limit pretty quickly. The loan limit is the number of properties your bank will allow you to finance. This is somewhere between four to 10. You can try applying at other banks but they're unlikely to approve you since your debt to income ratio will be too high. You'll learn about this ratio in the chapter on financing.

With loans limited to this level you cannot invest in more than four to six properties at once, for the most part. This limits your earning and appreciation potential.

The best investments usually require a little rehab upfront. Perhaps the paint is chipped or the exterior needs a good jet wash.

Rehabbing a single family home tends to cost a lot more than a multi-unit complex. This is because tenants tend to stay in single family homes for a lot longer and as a result, there's more damage to deal with. Your costs will likely run into the thousands depending on how long the family has stayed there. This happens even with the best tenant. Often, appliances will be out of date and won't appeal to new tenants and this adds to your costs.

While good deals exist everywhere, you'll be fighting a larger pool of investors to locate good deals on single family homes. With everyone competing for the same type of property it can be tough to score a great bargain. You might have to push your boundaries a little bit in order to score a good deal. This doesn't mean it's

impossible. It's just that you need to work a lot harder than investors in other types of properties.

Overall, single family homes can be great in terms of stability. However, that very stability creates issues that you'll need to account for.

Multifamily Properties

As the name suggests, multifamily properties contain more than one unit within the building. It could be a duplex with two units or a large apartment complex.

These types of properties usually attract seasoned real estate investors since they're more intimidating to manage.

This isn't necessarily the case because, with smart processes, even beginners can score great deals.

A case in point is the house hacking strategy where the owner lives in one unit and rents the rest out. These types of investors are usually first timers and it's fully possible to make this a success. Multifamily properties can be either small or large. Small properties typically contain less than four units within them. Larger properties usually have above this number.

Whatever the number of units are, the decision to invest in a property should come down to the numbers it can produce for you. Don't be intimidated by the number of units or think that a property is simply too "big" and disqualify it. The classification of large and small does matter to lending firms though.

Typically, large properties are considered commercial ones and the financing terms change dramatically. It's tougher to get financing for them unless you have decent experience investing in properties prior to that. Small properties are considered residential and therefore attract better financing terms.

Commercial properties are also valued differently from residential ones. In the case of small multifarities and single family residences, the price of a property is determined by what a comparable property in the neighborhood sold for. This is usually referred to as a comp.

With commercial properties, the return on investment is far more important and is compared to other properties in the neighborhood.

The return an investor could earn is calculated by dividing the income earned through rentals by the overall value of the property. This is called the capitalization or cap rate of a property. The higher the cap rate, the more valuable the property is. Commercial or not, multifarities provide more cash flow possibilities.

They're also likely to be turnkey projects. A turnkey is a rental property that generates cash flow from the first day. A multifamily unit tends to be easier to place on rent since the cost of renting tends to be lower than a single family home. The other advantage is that a small increase in rent can boost the overall cash flow by a large amount. This, in turn, can reduce per unit expenses even more and you'll earn more money from it.

Another advantage is that when you finance such a property you'll need to apply for just one loan. By investing in multifamily properties you don't need to worry about applying for a new loan every single time you purchase a property.

One loan gives you access to at least two units and one insurance policy covers all of them.

The point about insurance is something you'll realize when you begin to administer your properties. These policies generate the largest amount of paperwork. If you have 10 separate units, the paperwork is going to be monumental. Instead, with a multifamily property you could have 10 units and just one policy to worry about.

These properties also make it easier for an investor to focus on the numbers and not get caught up with the emotion of owning a property. You're not tied to a single family that's living there for a long time. Your tenants come and go and your properties are cash generating machines that exist to make you money. It's easier to treat such investments as a business and not as a hobby. They're easier to manage as well since you're more likely to find a management company to take care of it for you as opposed to a single family home where you'll need to take care of everything.

When the time comes to exit your investment you'll find that it's easier to boost the value of the property by modifying your costs and rental cash flow. This is because the appraisal, especially for large properties, is done on the basis of ROI and not on comps. Therefore, you can boost the value of your property by reducing your costs and increasing rents.

This is a lot easier to do with multifamily properties than with a single family residence where the quality of the property only matters if it happens to be worse than those around it.

There's also less competition to deal with from other investors. Most people simply don't bid on multifamily properties since these don't fit the American Dream stereotype. These properties don't have a place for the dog to run around or for a baby room to be created. There is, also, usually no separate garage or similar amenities.

It's all about the math and as an investor, this is a great thing for you. Their valuations are more objective and you can derive them a lot more easily than with single family properties.

Disadvantages

The biggest disadvantage of investing in multifamily properties is that they can be expensive to buy. While their per unit costs are low, the overall prices increase when you're dealing with more than four units.

This is a significant barrier of entry for most people. This ensures lower competition for properties, of course, so there is a positive side to this.

The presence of multiple units makes these properties more intense to manage. For the most part, investors choose to outsource management to professional companies since managing it themselves would be close to impossible. The tenants who occupy these units will also create more headaches for you than the ones who occupy single family homes.

Since the units are smaller, the tenants view these places as being transitory and take less care of the premises. They're also more likely to be late on their rental payments and will complain for pettier reasons.

As long as the investor has outsourced management to another company, they won't have to deal with this alone. However, outsourcing costs money and reduces ROI.

While competition for multifamily properties is lower, the competition tends to be more sophisticated.

Often, they'll have more money than you and this might cause you to lose out on a few deals since you simply cannot hope to compete against them.

The investment itself tends to be more complicated and contains more moving parts. Flipping such properties is very risky, for example, since rehab costs per unit can easily spiral out of control.

There are also fewer properties to choose like this since they're not as much in demand as single family homes are. A lot of these deals involve syndication. This is when the investor raises money from other people and invests in the property on behalf of a syndicate. This raises the question of governmental regulation. If you don't adhere to those rules you'll likely end up in white collar prison.

The choice of investing in a single family or multi family is a tricky one. My advice is to start off slow and invest in a single family property or in a small multi family unit while occupying one of the units yourself. This will let you know what the issues are and you can earn a pretty good return. Once you've managed to save enough cash from your first investment, you can choose where you'd like to invest next since you'll know whether you're willing to live with the disadvantages of each type of investment.

Condos

Condos can come in the form of single family or multi family residences. A condo stands for condominium and, from the outside, these can look like apartment complexes. The difference is that in an apartment complex, a single owner leases out the individual units. In a condo complex, every unit is owned individually by an owner. A single person can own two or more condos but generally, each unit has a different owner.

The common areas are owned by the homeowner's association (HOA) and they collect a fee for upkeep and maintenance. Owning a condo for rental purposes can reduce your costs. For example, maintenance costs are typically lower since the HOA will take care of these. However, there are some additional rules and regulations you should watch out for.

The first is that some HOAs don't allow owners to rent their premises out to tenants during the first two years of ownership. This sounds ridiculous since they're dictating what you can do with your property, but it is fully legal. The best thing to do is to check the rules as outlined in the condominium map which is the official name for the rulebook that the HOA produces.

You will be liable for the HOA fee and these can be hefty depending on the property. You'll need to include this before calculating your ROI.

The HOA is all powerful in a condo complex and the worst thing that can happen is for a person with a thirst for control getting onto the board.

They can turn your life into a living hell should they choose and you'll have to play by their rules.

It's helpful to take the time to get to know the people who live in the complex and some of the other owners. They'll have a say in how you use your property. For example, if you decide to rent it out on Airbnb, the HOA has the right to stop you from doing this.

There are also occasional special assessment fees that the HOA charges from time to time.

These are fees needed for upgrades to the property that the HOA cannot cover with the regular fees alone. These can eat into your returns, so it's worthwhile to budget for these ahead of time. Condo prices swing wildly in urban areas due to varying demand for them. While some people prefer living in a community where everyone is invested in everyone else's mutual benefit, some HOAs can be tyrannical, and this causes everyone to jump ship.

This doesn't mean you should stay away from condos. My aim is to present all sides of the issue here. There are excellent rental properties that happen to be condos.

Take the time to understand all aspects of your investment before choosing to invest.

Another type of property that is very similar to a condo is a townhome. These are usually multiple units that are separately owned but exist within the same building. These don't feel like apartments and instead give off a detached single family home vibe. They're wall to wall with the adjacent unit and typically consist of multiple floors, but they are most similar to condos in how they operate.

Real Estate Owner Properties (REOs)

An REO is a property that is owned by the bank or by the local government. These are homes that have been foreclosed upon or have been vacant for many years. In the past, REOs used to proceed to auction or they could be bought directly from a bank's listings. These days, though, banks are increasingly placing them for sale on the Multiple Listing System (MLS) which is a network that all realtors use to list homes and locate deals.

As a rental property investor, you will likely find that the majority of your investments will be REOs. The only exception is if you're investing in turnkey properties. REO properties usually have some damage in the form of mold or infestation. They need some money to be put into them in order for the investor to get value out of them.

Many investors don't want to deal with these issues and stay away from them. This gives you a great way to locate great deals.

Having said that, it's also easy to land a real stinker that has no hope of paying off your investment. The thing to do is to be careful when evaluating these properties.

A major advantage of buying REOs is that you'll be dealing with professional sellers in the form of banks. Banks have an in-built incentive to let these go because they're not in the business of managing properties. They want to earn interest on loans and the longer a property stays on their books, the more non performing assets they have.

Therefore, banks will not be offended if you offer a lowball price. They might ask you to come back with a better offer but you don't have to worry about offending them and them not dealing with you ever again. That's something you'll need to look out for when dealing with individuals.

Rehabbers

These kinds of properties are what most beginners to real estate investing think of when someone tells them to invest in properties. Everyone loves a good transformation and houses are no different. The idea with a rehabber is to locate a property that is in distress and turn it into something that can be rented out. There are many advantages as well as disadvantages to investing in a property that needs rehab.

First off, understand that properties need different levels of rehab.

Some might need some paint and new lights while others might need certain parts of the property torn down. It's not as if the worse the property is, the better your deal can be. Sometimes, there's a good reason a property is in as bad a shape as it is.

It might be a better idea to tear it down and build something else on the land.

However, due to the perceived difficulty of valuing such properties, you'll find less competition. This is especially the case with single family homes since most buyers will be occupying their properties instead of using it for cash flow. No one wants a project and you will be one of the few who can bid on such properties. This makes finding a deal pretty easy.

Once you put work into the property you'll be surprised at how much it can appreciate. This is called the ARV or After Repair Value. It isn't uncommon to see price appreciations of 30% or more after repairs are conducted. That is a massive gain and it supercharges your capital gains. This is why most home flippers [who invest in rehabs] sell the property since the money they earn can be massive.

If you hold onto the property, your rental yields will be massive. For example, let's say you bought a property for $50,000 and invested $10,000 into it for repairs. You financed this deal by paying 20% of the price upfront so your down payment was $10,000.

Your total cash investment in the deal is the down payment plus the rehab cost which is ($10,000+$10,000) $20,000.

Let's say the property value increases by 30% after repairs. This means the ARV is (50000*1.3) = $65,000. You own 20% of the ARV, so your equity in the property is 20% of $65,000 which is $13,000. You've created an equity gain of $3,000 for yourself. Your ROI is this gain amount divided by the cash you invested. This is (3000/20000) 15%.

Now let's say you earn a rental amount of $650 per month from this property.

Your rental yield is calculated by dividing the yearly rental amounts earned by the price you paid for the property. This is (650*12)/(58000) 13.4%. If someone buys the property at the ARV value, they'd earn (650*12)/(65000) 12% per year. You're earning an additional 1.4% because you invested in a rehab.

If these numbers cause your head to spin, it highlights one of the negatives of investing in rehabs. They're very number sensitive and most beginners tend to stay away from them. You need to have a good feel for ROI calculations and proper offer prices to succeed at making rehabs work. Don't worry though, all of this can be learned.

I'll be giving you simple rules of thumb that will make your life a lot easier and you'll be able to figure these numbers out easily.

One of the other disadvantages of investing in rehabs is that traditional banks will not touch them. You'll need to get creative with your financing. This means approaching a hard money lender. This is both an advantage and a disadvantage. Hard money lenders can offer you amazing terms.

For example, if you're well known to them and have done business in the past, they will be willing to offer you zero money down loans and will finance the entire property themselves. However, they're also likely to turn around and ask you to pay 40% down at an exorbitant interest rate. They will charge higher than normal interest rates compared to traditional banks since they're assuming greater risks.

What rehabbers do is use a bridge loan. The bridge loan is money lent by a hard money lender that is used to spruce up the property and get in a fit shape. The rehabber then turns around and refinances the property with a traditional bank. Since the property is in great shape and is being rented out, the bank won't have any qualms financing it.

Since the value of the property has risen, the loan amount from the bank usually covers the amount the hard money lender

has paid as well as compensates the investor for the cash they put into the project. They thus manage to get their money out of the property and can invest it elsewhere.

This is a pretty stressful way of making money. What if the bank does not agree to refinance the property? What if the investor rips a wall open and finds an even bigger issue lurking behind it?

There are a lot of hidden expenses that crop up and it's tough for a new investor to accurately estimate costs.

Beginners are best off sticking to simple properties that need cosmetic changes to them. Leave the hardcore rehabs for later once you have enough capital and can estimate repairs better. It's a bit unrealistic to expect to make a rehabber work if you have a full time job. You need to have the time to attend to all the issues that will crop up. You'll also need to have a strong network of contractors to call in case things go wrong.

Commercial Properties

Commercial property investing is a different ball game from residential investments. A commercial property is one that is leased to someone (either an individual or a company) that uses the space for work purposes. It's tougher to obtain financing for commercial properties but the profits can be higher.

A lot of the terms of commercial leases can be adjusted. Many commercial leases offer the landlord a cut of their tenant's revenues. Other leases are structured to be triple net. A triple net lease is one where the tenant is responsible for almost every expense except taxes on the property. Remodeling, maintenance, etc fall on the tenant. This makes owning the property extremely passive. However, the returns are lower as well.

Something to keep in mind when renting commercial property is that you will need a whole host of liability insurance policies. This is because if someone gets hurt on your premises, the landlord could be held accountable. There are other issues that crop up as well and, generally speaking, this makes commercial property investment unsafe for beginners.

Chapter 4 Location Analysis

It's no secret that the success of your real estate investment depends on the location of your property. Different locations call for different types of investment. Contrary to popular perception, it's more than possible to invest in so-called "expensive" markets such

as New York and the Northeast and make a profit.

Understand your location well and you'll know exactly how to go about turning a profit from your investment. The first thing for you to understand are neighborhood classes.

Classes

Neighborhoods receive grades just like you did when in school or college. There are four grades that are given: A, B, C and D. I must mention that these classes aren't fixed by the government or some other organization. Instead, it's something that all real estate investors refer to when talking amongst themselves.

This means the lines that divide the categories aren't clear. However, the objective of these classes isn't to exactly determine what kind of a property you're investing in. Instead, it's to help you ballpark the type of property you're looking at. If someone brings you a lead and tells you that they've found a B property in an A neighborhood you immediately know what to look for.

Neighborhoods and properties can receive different grades depending on their characteristics. The important thing is to understand the broad categories and what they indicate instead of trying to pinpoint a property's category with a high level of accuracy. Differences of opinion will crop up. You might think of a property as being a B while someone else might think it's a D.

Some investors use different grading scales as well. They might use just three grades while others might use grades up to F.

Grade A

These locations have the newest buildings, the best entertainment options, the wealthiest people, and the highest costing properties. If you're talking about buildings, the same theme follows. These buildings are new, have excellent maintenance records, and have almost no issues in sight.

They're chock full of features that a high end consumer will demand such as high end appliances, spotless countertops, hardwood floors and so on. These properties command the highest rent.

However, their cash flow might not be the highest because they will demand more maintenance and upkeep. Your tenants will be extremely discerning and you'll have to work extra hard to keep them satisfied.

I'm not saying these properties don't make great investments. It's just that you need to understand the way they work. Often people confuse a property they would love to live in for one that would be a great investment. When evaluating investments, always stick to the numbers. How you feel about it is neither here nor there.

Grade B

B locations are slightly older than As. However, they're still good neighborhoods and have good entertainment options. The schools in them are considered very good if not elite. These areas typically run middle to upper middle class. There might be some people who live paycheck to paycheck in them, but they won't be as concentrated here.

A B building follows the same logic. B buildings will usually be between 15 to 30 years old and will be upgraded for the most part. They won't have the shiny new gleam of an A building but they'll be very respectable.

Rental income is lower but cash flow might be higher. However, some of these buildings might have impending maintenance issues that will put a dent in your pocket.

Grade C

A C neighborhood is usually lower income and is populated by lower middle class to families that are slightly above the poverty line. The average person living here probably works a low wage job and is probably living off government subsidies.

Take a look at the commercial stores in the area and you'll see a lot of liquor stores and cash advance places. Pawn shops are also prevalent around here.

The buildings in such neighborhoods are usually older than 30 years and they haven't been maintained very well. A lot of repairs will be needed and the internal systems such as plumbing and wiring will require attention. The rental amounts will be low, but the properties will be quite affordable.

Class D

A D neighborhood is one you would visit only if you were kidnapped. This might sound harsh but these neighborhoods are the ones you avoid at all costs. It's where the poorest of the poor live and crime, drugs and violence is a daily problem.

Police patrols will be common here and convenience stores will likely have screens that prevent clerks from being shot.

Not every city or region has a D neighborhood so that's of some solace. Look for the presence of boarded up vacant properties and condemned buildings. A D building is usually very old. They will need a huge amount of repairs to make them even slightly respectable.

The tenants you'll attract will also often be living paycheck to paycheck. The good news is that these properties will be dirt cheap and will often be attached to some government subsidy. Many cities have programs to spruce up their inner city areas and investors will receive special financing for such properties. This doesn't mean you should take it but it might help your cash flow quite a bit.

Again, these categories are fluid and depend on your own discretion. You'll need to mix and match what sorts of properties you're looking at. Turnkey rental investors typically look at A properties in B areas or As in A areas. Those who prefer to rehab properties might look for B buildings in C areas and so on.

Crime

The one thing that drives away great tenants more than anything else is crime. High crime areas will make your life hell as a property owner since you'll probably be called regularly to address gunshots in the middle of the night. This is the first thing you should check when trying to grade an area or building.

Here are some excellent resources to help you figure out the crime situation (Turner, 2016):

crimereports.com

neighborhoodscout.com

city-data.com usa.com/rank

Of these, the second option is paid, but the rest are free. If you live in the area where your property is, you'll probably have a good idea of where the crime infested zones are. All of these resources provide you with a map of where the crime hotspots occur. Needless to say, you want to stay on the right side of the tracks when looking at properties.

It's always best to tour the community in person. Maps don't show the invisible lines that exist in communities. For example, many inner city areas are restricted to a few blocks of town. Residents might avoid those areas and live just one block away from them since the perception of that block might be very different. These invisible lines play an important role in determining what kind of tenants you attract to your property.

Drug Use

Drug abuse is harder to pinpoint. Generally speaking, the higher crime areas have problems with drug addiction. However, this has been changing of late thanks to the opioid crisis where residents of seemingly clean neighborhoods have been exposed to drug use problems. The best way to determine the extent of the issue is to visit the neighborhood in person and talk to the businesses there.

Local grocers and police officers on patrol are the best sources of information. You can also read what people are saying about the neighborhood online by looking at the rental listings in the area. If you see a high prevalence of rental listings for entire units increasing over time then it's an indicator that some issues have been cropping up.

Schools

Schools are a great shortcut to figuring out the quality of a neighborhood. A great neighborhood has great schools. This makes sense since parents want to give their children the best education possible. The proximity of a good school nearby drives property

values up and automatically ensures the neighborhood will be a good one.

This doesn't always work out, but it's a good way to begin your search. A good resource to use when evaluating schools is greatschools.org. This website provides a rating for all schools on a scale of one to 10 with one being the worst.

Unemployment

Unemployment is a tricky thing to determine since the national and local statistics imply different things. While a national unemployment rate of around 10% is very bad, a similar unemployment rate in a local area isn't quite so. Local real estate prices and economies aren't always directly connected to the national picture so you need to take location factors into account.

Areas with high employment rates might not always prove to be the best ones to invest in. If all the employment in the area is generated by a single firm or factory then this is a potentially bad situation for you. What if the company packs up? The entire town could go under and you'll have a D property on your hands overnight.

This is precisely what happened to the smaller towns in the midwest once the steel mills and car factories started shipping jobs overseas. You want to stay well away from such situations. You might find a local area that has a 10% unemployment rate. This equally implies that 90% of the people living there are employed. This is a very good thing.

Therefore, you need to be more careful when screening tenants. As long as employment isn't dependent on one particular industry or company, you can live with some level of unemployment. To find unemployment statistics, head over to city- data.com. You could also try the U.S Department of Labor's website which publishes local level data on a zip code basis.

Population

Growing populations support growing rents. This is simply the law of supply and demand in action. The problem is that evaluating population growth is even tougher than figuring out employment statistics. Your best bet is to head over to usa.com/rank and look at where your prospective area lands on the list of growing population zones.

A stable population is also a good thing. What you want to stay away from at all costs is a declining population. This points to some local issue that will become a bigger problem as time moves on.

A good way to estimate population growth is to look at housing starts and building permits data.

You can view this data for free at census.gov/construction/nrc. That's the U.S Census Bureau's website and it has data regarding building permit applications.

A paid source is the National Association of Home Builders at nahb.org. Areas that are declining in population will see lower housing starts.

They're not fully correlated however. It is possible for an area to experience an oversupply of homes which will lead to more vacancies down the line.

Transportation and Local Businesses

Does the area you're looking at have good access to transportation? If there's a light rail nearby, chances are that the area has some degree of prosperity to it. This is because people use these options to travel to and from work. If there is no public transport, how good is the highway infrastructure?

Rural areas can have good investments, but their desolate nature makes it tough for people to commute to their jobs. Those jobs pay them money that they use to pay you rents. So, it's in your interest to look for properties that are close to good transportation options.

Another key indicator of an area's quality is the type of local businesses operating there. If a major chain like Starbucks decides to open an outlet, they've probably done the research to determine their market. If you see a preponderance of Taco Bells and KFCs, then you know you're looking at a lower income neighborhood.

These local businesses also provide your tenants with good entertainment options that make your property a better place to live.

Buy something out in the middle of nowhere and you'll likely find that your tenants don't stay there for long because there's nothing to do.

Rental Yields

This is a great metric that can help you quickly figure out the profit potential of investing in a particular area. The best part is that all the data you need is completely free online. Head over to Zillow.com/research/data to download the data for all zip codes. They have data that lists the median sales price as well as the monthly rental amounts.

You'll need to download this data into an excel file and search for your zip code. Once this is done, calculate the rental yield. First, multiply the monthly rental payment by 12. This gives you the yearly rental amount. Divide this by the median home value to get the rental yield.

As a rule of thumb you want to look at areas that are over 11%.

Some investors look at areas that offer 24% or more, although these are rare and require some form of rehabbing.

I'll explain this rule in more detail in the next chapter. Keep in mind that this data doesn't take the nature of the local neighborhood into account.

Some zip codes have a mix of B and C neighborhoods while some have a mix of A and C in them.

Each neighborhood is different, so take this into account.

A good way to narrow down your search is to look for zip codes that offer at least eight percent yields. This doesn't mean you won't find bargains in other places, but it does give you a better chance of finding something profitable in the long term.

You'll probably need to force appreciation to generate substantial cash flow from those properties. Take a look at your new list of zip codes and you can analyze them for neighborhood mix. Another great way to figure out rental yields is to look at rental listings in the area.

There are many websites that contain these, the most popular being Craigslist. This will help you figure out the different parts of the zip code and you can see how the yields vary. Keep in mind that if you see a bunch of listings pop up in a short period of time this indicates something is going wrong over there.

This is why the best way to evaluate a neighborhood is to visit it in person and speak to the people who live and work there.

Vacancy Rates

Vacancy rates aren't referring to the number of vacant homes in an area. It's the average length of time properties lie unoccupied. As a landlord, having a vacant property is one of the biggest expenses you'll have to incur.

While it's great to imagine your property being occupied all the time, this isn't very realistic. This is especially the case if you own a multifamily property.

The best way to figure out an area's vacancy rate is to contact local property management companies. Some people will tell you to check out the U.S Census Bureau's statistics, but this data isn't always immediately accessible.

Instead, talk to the people who deal with properties directly. This means landlords and property management companies are your best bet.

Normally, they would know the numbers you'll need and you'll obtain the information quickly. You'll need to account for vacancies in your calculations. I'll show you how to do this in the next chapter. The average vacancy rate in the U.S hovers around seven percent, but this is a national number. Local numbers vary.

You might be wondering what a good vacancy rate is. The answer is that there is no such thing. As long as the rate is something sensible, you'll have to work around it. For example, if properties in an area are vacant 30% of the time, this is a huge number and it'll be hard to overcome this hurdle.

The usual way that landlords overcome vacancies is to charge slightly higher rents to compensate for the times the property will be empty. However, there's a limit to how much you can charge someone.

Always assume the worst case scenario when calculating your numbers.

You can reduce the impact of vacancies by managing your property well. By attracting high quality tenants and offering them payment plans, it is possible to reduce your vacancy rate to as low as two percent on multifamily properties.

However, estimating the worst case scenario in your calculations is the best thing to do.

Insurance and Taxes

Check the property tax rates in the area when performing your calculations. Some areas such as the Denver metropolitan area have low rates. Anything in the northeast has high property tax rates. Florida has low rates and so on. You'll pay property taxes once a year, but it can cut into your profits so make sure you account for them.

Something else that needs accounting but most homeowners miss is insurance. Regular insurance policies add to your costs. If you pay less than 20% down on a property, you'll have to pay mortgage insurance every month and this adds significant costs to your overall cash flow over the course of the loan term.

Keep in mind that regular homeowner's insurance doesn't cover events such as floods and hurricanes. Florida might have low tax rates but you'll have to pay for hurricane insurance.

If you happen to be looking at properties in the greater Houston area, you'll have to get flood insurance. Flood insurance is something that every homeowner complains about but when a flood hits, but they're always extremely thankful they bought it.

Flood insurance is particularly expensive and is currently subsidized by the government as a stop gap measure. The future rates might increase so this is an unknown at the moment. They also have high deductibles, so if your damage doesn't exceed that amount, the insurance might not even help you. However, it will help you avoid complete disaster.

Should you avoid investing in properties that are in a floodplain? There's no easy answer to this. You can find some real bargains with such properties if fewer investors want them. However, this is balanced by the increased costs and probability that you will have to deal with a disaster at some point. Make sure you check with the financing institution how a writeoff in case of a flood will be dealt with. Run the numbers fully before deciding what to do.

Take all of the factors outlined in this chapter into account when evaluating the location of your property investment. There is no definitive method of doing this. Every situation is different. what's important is for you to understand both the risks and opportunities present in a situation.

Chapter 5 Sourcing Great Deals

Now should you go about finding good deals and is it even possible for a new investor to compete with the established players? These are the two most common questions new real estate investors ask themselves. The answer is that there are many ways to find great deals and that it is fully possible for you to find good

deals ahead of experienced investors.

This doesn't mean every deal you'll find will be a great one. You can always pass on the ones you don't like. The first thing for you to figure out is to understand what a good deal even looks like. I'm not talking about the condition of the property or even the location. While those are important, the most important thing is the numbers.

If the numbers don't make sense, there's no point trying to make a deal work for you. Running the numbers doesn't require you to input everything into a spreadsheet and run a cost benefit analysis. There are some handy rules of thumb that you're going to learn which will shortcut the process for you.

At some point you will need to run a detailed numerical analysis.

This point is usually reached once you've already bought the property since it's impossible to know exact numbers beforehand. Figuring out your income from the property is quite straightforward. You need rental income to exceed expenses. Some property owners don't include the mortgage expense in this calculation.

This makes sense in areas where rental payments do not cover mortgage expenses. As a beginner, it's best for you to aim for a situation where your income after maintenance and other expenses covers mortgage payments. This way, you won't be creating a cash flow hold for yourself. Also, make sure you have enough cash in the bank to cover at least six months' worth of mortgage payments before buying the property.

As you can see, there is considerable planning that needs to occur before you start searching. For starters, have at least 20% of the property's price as cash on hand.

Once you find suitable properties (using the methods I'll show you later in this chapter) you can estimate the mortgage payment using the calculator at: https://www.bankrate.com/calculators/mortgages/mortgage- calculator.aspx.

You'll have a rough idea of the rental income you can earn thanks to the location analysis you'll have carried out. If the mortgage payment isn't covered by the rental payment, you need to increase your down payment amount until it does so. There are also maintenance and vacancy expenses to consider. Is your head spinning yet? Well, this is where the following rules of thumb come into play!

Two Simple Rules of Thumb

Estimating expenses and figuring out the right offer price are two things that often intimidate new investors. They rightly identify that these two things do more than anything else to determine the profitability of their deal. Without landlording experience though, it's tough to correctly estimate these numbers. Get it wrong and you'll be stuck with a 30 year mistake.

Let's deal with estimating expenses first. This is done by the one percent rule.

The One Percent Rule

How can you make sure the property you're looking at will generate enough income to cover all conceivable expenses and still leave you with enough to cover the mortgage payment? The one percent rule helps you figure this out. Search for properties that will provide you with monthly rental income that is one percent of the property's overall value.

If the property you're looking at is worth $200,000 then the monthly rental payment must be one percent of this or $2,000 at the very least. This equates to $24,000 per year or a 12% yield.

You won't earn this entire amount, of course, since expenses will eat away at it. How do you estimate expenses?

This can be done using the 50% rule. This rule states that your expenses will be half of your rental income per month. This means, in our example above, you'll earn $1,000 per month after accounting for maintenance, vacancies, property management, taxes and insurance. It's a rough estimate, but it works very well when looked at on an annual basis.

This leaves you with $1,000 to cover mortgage expenses. Is this enough? Well, let's use the calculator linked above to figure this out. I'm going to assume an interest rate of 3.1% for a 30 year mortgage. Plugging in the value of the property as $200,000 and the down payment at 20% ($40,000) this gives us a monthly payment of $889. This is great! You have $1,000 leftover after expenses and this covers all expenses. However, $40,000 might seem like a lot.

So, how low can you go on your down payment? Playing around with the down payment percentage, a three percent down payment ($6,000 upfront) gives us a monthly payment of $1,029.

This means you'll have to pay $29 out of pocket every month. If you put 10% down ($20,000) you'll have to pay $969 every month. This puts money in your pocket.

Needless to say not all assumptions might hold water. Your interest rate might be different and you could have a tough time locating properties that fit the one percent rule. There's no denying that using the rule shortcuts your calculation process massively.

What if you can't find ready to rent properties that don't satisfy the one percent rule? In this scenario, you'll have to search for properties that require a little fixing. This makes your offer price extremely important. Truth be told, most great rental deals are found by looking at REOs and these always need some fixing up.

How can you figure out a sensible offer price?

The 70 Percent Rule

The 70 percent rule helps you figure out what a sensible offer price is. It's used by home flippers all the time and works very well. It states that you should offer 70% of the ARV minus the cost of rehab for the deal to make sense. Let's say you spot a property that needs some fixing up and is currently selling for $150,000.

You estimate that with $10,000 worth of repairs, the ARV will rise to $200,000. At this point, you can earn

$2,000 per month in rental income. This property easily satisfies the one percent rule since you're acquiring it for $160,000 (the home value plus the rehab costs of $10,000). So how much should you offer?

The 70 percent rule states that we need to first subtract rehab costs from the ARV. This leaves us with $190,000. Now, we offer 70% of this value which is $133,000. This helps us account for any unexpected expenses. If the seller accepts this offer (a bank usually will) you'll have a property that is easily fulfilling the one percent rule.

The catch here is that you need to correctly estimate the ARV. This is easily done. All you need to do is talk to an agent or look at existing sale listings. You need to correctly estimate rehab costs but you've built a decent cushion for yourself. It's a good idea to have 50% of estimated rehab costs as cash on hand. Then, there's financing.

Traditional banks might not finance this property. You'll have to approach a hard money lender. They might require a higher down payment and a higher interest rate. It depends on how the negotiation goes. You can use the calculator linked previously and play around with the numbers to see if the deal makes sense.

As a beginner, it's best to stick to properties that need some cosmetic changes. A lick of paint, some new cabinets, better door handles and locks, and a good clean. These expenses will be low and while the ARV boost won't be high, you'll manage to clear the one percent hurdle easily. Banks will also be willing to finance properties that don't need too much work and this makes it even easier for you to turn a profit.

These two rules, the one percent and 70 percent, will make your life a whole lot easier. Once you have the property on hand you will need to run the numbers again to make sure your expenses are lining up in accordance to what you estimated. Remember that it's best to get paid to own an asset. From the one percent section, if you're being paid $29 per month this doesn't sound like much. However, you're being paid this to own a $200,000 asset that is appreciating all the time!

Deal Sources

Now that you know what the numbers on a good deal looks like, it's time to look at the sources that contain these deals. The first and best place to find them is the Multiple Listing System or MLS.

MLS

The MLS is an electronic network of sale listings. Each area and locality has its own MLS and these combine with one another to form a national MLS.

The negative here is that you won't have access to it unless you possess a real estate license. You will need to go through someone else, most probably an agent, to find properties that satisfy your needs.

This is annoying and my recommendation is to get your own license so that you can have access to the system. This way, you can respond quickly to properties the minute they hit the system. The MLS is quite competitive since experienced investors are very active on it and will respond with offers within the matter of a few hours.

How can you compete against this? The first step is to find a really good agent. This person needs to be motivated enough to send you listings. Next, you need to run the property through the rules of thumb I mentioned previously and figure out what your numbers look like.

It's helpful to meet with the agent beforehand and discuss your plans. They're experienced and will have a good idea of what will work best for you. That way, you won't waste each other's time. This will also allow you to screen out the deals that don't make sense to you. When it comes to the MLS, speed matters, so discuss what kind of a workflow will help you and the agent.

The other method to adopt is to look for old listings. These listings have been sitting there for a while and not all of them will be gems. However, there will be a few that will make sense for you. The best part is you can offer a lower amount since selling a property is a stressful experience. The seller will likely be worried about how long it's been sitting on the market and they're losing money every day it sits there.

Whichever approach you choose, you need to make a mental shift. You need to fail fast and often. That's right! If your offers are being accepted easily then it's a sign you're offering too much.

As a rule of thumb, a 10% success rate on your offers is too high. The key to success is placing a lot of offers and waiting for a response. The traditional thought process of finding a dream home and then offering a price and having it immediately accepted won't work here.

That's for people who don't understand what assets and liabilities are.

Stick to properties that need some value addition or need some work to be done. Talk to your agent and ask them to put you in touch with contractors. The contractor won't help you estimate costs without payment but talking to them will give you a feel for the prices of services.

Another method that works is to visit any big box store and look at the prices for paint and other common fixer upper items.

Talk to the salespeople at these stores since most of them will have contracting experience. You can show them photos and get a ballpark estimate. Do all of this with sample properties you don't plan on bidding. This way, you'll gain experience and can quickly respond when you do see something you like.

Something else to keep in mind is that you should minimize contingencies in your offer. A contingency is a clause that allows you to withdraw the offer. The most common contingency, and one that you should include, is an inspection contingency. It states that if you don't find any major issues upon inspection, your offer stands.

You should include a few contingencies, but don't go overboard. Your agent will help you figure out which ones ought to be included. Beginner investors typically include a ton of contingencies and sellers balk at this. After all, the more contingencies there are the higher the chance of a deal falling through. Keep your offer as clean as possible.

The MLS is extremely competitive and there's no denying that beginner investors are at a disadvantage. This means you need to get creative with your efforts.

Direct Mail Campaigns

Direct mail campaigns are something that wholesalers and home flippers conduct regularly. However, rental investors don't do it.

The reasons for avoiding this have never made sense to me personally. A direct mail campaign might sound antiquated but it works precisely because of that. It helps you stand out more in today's digital age.

The way wholesalers locate properties is to send a bunch of postcards repeatedly over the course of a year to prospective sellers.

By repeatedly, I don't mean they spam these people. They send perhaps one postcard every month. Sending mail repeatedly is what works best since a typical seller will not respond the first few times to a stranger's offer to buy their property.

Wholesalers treat the cost of sending mails as a business expense that they'll recover once they sell the property. Many rental investors hold onto their property for the long term and this is why the upfront cost of sending mail doesn't appeal to them. How will they recover their money? This is the wrong way to think about it.

Instead of looking at it as a separate cost, it's best to include it as a part of closing costs. That way, you'll be able to justify spending the money upfront. If you manage to locate a great deal, then the expense will be worth it. The people who typically sell their homes and respond to direct mail requests are generally those who are in special situations.

These people are either individuals going through specific financial circumstances or have inherited a property that they're not interested in maintaining anymore.

There are also landlords who haven't been able to make a success of their investment and are stuck with a deadbeat tenant.

Such listings never make it onto the MLS and it's where you'll find great bargains. You need to work a little to find these opportunities but once you do, it'll be worth it. The question is, how do you increase your chances of finding such people? The best way to begin is to send feelers out to absentee owners. These are people who don't live in their properties.

You can purchase these lists from listsource.com and melissadata.com. Send letters or postcards to the people on these lists once every month or quarter and wait for replies. No one can guarantee replies but again, this is a numbers game. If you send 1,000 postcards in one go, let's say 50 people respond. If you manage to locate two good deals out of this 50, that's two deals per month which is more than enough to keep you occupied.

Some wholesalers even tape signs all over a neighborhood but this is a pretty cheap way to advertise. The kinds of properties you'll be called about will match the level of your advertising. They'll require a lot of work and won't make sense for a beginner investor.

So be patient throughout this process and send postcards or letters out regularly.

Driving

Your car costs money every month so why not put it to good use and use it to make you money? If you've had your eye on a neighborhood, why not drive around in it to take a look at the properties that could potentially be a good investment?

As is the case with direct mail, this is a numbers game, so don't expect to find hidden gold mines every time you do this.

The types of properties you want to look for are those that are in a state of neglect. Full mailboxes, uncut grass, broken windows, and so on. While you want to stay away from properties that are of the C and D type, you can take a chance on them if the neighborhood is good enough.

Take pictures of the property and note down the address. You can look up the address in the county office's tax records department and send the owner a letter offering to buy their property. There will even be a phone number listed so you can call them as well.

Evictions

As a landlord, you're going to have to deal with evictions at some point. I won't sugar coat anything, they're a nightmare to deal with. You'll have a crazy tenant, a dirty property and you're going to have to spend money to clean the place. This is pretty much the experience that every landlord deals with. It also spells opportunity for you.

Some landlords would rather saw their arm off than deal with an eviction. You can step in and offer a low price to deal with the problem. They'll usually be happy to get rid of it if they're motivated enough. The question is, how can you get a hold of a list of evictions? The answer is public records.

County offices have records of eviction notices and a simple glance at these will give you the contact information of the landlord. Call them up and get to know the situation. Take a look at the property and allow a nice cushion for yourself in terms of rehab costs. Make them an offer and solve the situation.

Needless to say, you'll be taking on an unpleasant situation but it's worth taking the time if the numbers make sense to you. Every county has a different way of dealing with evictions so ask around in your local real estate investment club. Someone will have dealt with an eviction in there and you'll manage to learn about the process.

Craigslist

Craigslist has been around forever and is often thought of as a haven for renters. However, it's a great place to find sellers as well. The trick is to use the website correctly. The most passive and obvious way is to search the sale listings and to look if any property makes sense for you.

The less obvious way is to look at the rental listings and contact owners who are managing their properties themselves. You'll find a lot of listings being made by management companies so you want to stay away from these. They're not authorized to deal with sales after all.

Most landlords want to get rid of their property since they either haven't maintained it well enough or haven't taken the time to run the numbers properly. Tell them you're an investor and are interested in buying their property. You'll find properties that need some work and this is a great way to find bargains.

Another great way to use the website is to post an ad saying you'll buy homes. This might not lead to many serious responses but you never know where your next lead will come from. Craigslist is a great way to find bargains on unadvertised properties and you should be using it.

Find Wholesalers

Real estate wholesaling is a roller coaster and it takes a special type of person to succeed.

The way wholesaling works is someone finds a great property and then sells it to you for a higher price. As you can imagine, wholesalers aren't finding properties that are listed for market average prices.

They need to find properties selling at a deep discount in order to make a profit. They do this by assigning you the sales deed. An assignment occurs when one party transfers the contract to someone else at a small markup. For example, the wholesaler will locate a property for $50,000, assign it to you for $60,000 and collect a $10,000 profit. Your money will be used to pay the seller and you get the property once the title agent transfers it to you (more on this in the next chapter).

As you can see, the wholesaler needs to deal with a lot of moving parts. Many of them get chased away by sellers once they're sniffed out as a wholesaler since the seller knows they don't have the money. A good wholesaler will typically ask you for proof of funds. You can provide either a bank statement or a mortgage pre-approval letter that you'll learn about in the next chapter.

The wholesaler can then negotiate in good faith and deliver deals right to you. You can get in touch with wholesalers by calling numbers on bandit signs. These are the signs that say "we buy houses" or "we buy ugly homes" and so on. I must mention that a lot of wholesalers are in it because they've been sold the concept as being an easy way to get rich quickly.

You'll therefore meet many amateurs who have no idea what they're doing. It's best to have a few of them running around on your behalf. You can also train your own wholesaler and offer them a commission on the deals they bring in. This way, you can make sure they're bringing in the right properties.

Real estate clubs are usually full of these people so hang around one long enough and you'll meet them. Wholesalers can either be a waste of time or a great way to locate deals. Combine all of the methods discussed in this chapter and you'll have a smooth machine that will bring you deals regularly.

Chapter 6 Financing 101

This is the chapter that will save you the largest number of headaches. Financing is what most people dread and with good reason. There's no predicting how banks will react to your application and they always seem to demand mountains of paperwork. Many people go through the entire process only to find themselves being rejected.

There are many options that are available to you, but before understanding all of them, you need to learn how the process works. This process is similar for pretty much every option so let's take some time to look at what lenders' motivations are and how you can increase your odds of approval.

Process

The first step to obtaining financing isn't the application. It's preparation. You need to gather all kinds of documents that prove you aren't a deadbeat. The definition of deadbeat from a bank's perspective is different from what you might think. They're only interested in lending money to someone who can pay them back.

Banks make money on the interest you pay them after borrowing money.

They don't want you to pay your loans back early since this decreases their profits. Pay them back in a predictable manner and they'll rush to offer you more money. The key to all of this is to be prepared. For starters, gather the following documents:

A letter from your employer stating how long you've worked there and that you continue to perform your duties admirably

Salary stubs going back as long as you can manage to find them. Two years is a good period.

Tax records

Bank statements for the last year

Any other investment account statements such as brokerage statements or retirement account balance statements

Records of any other loans you currently have. Car loans, student loans etc.

Any other document that proves you're financially stable. For example, another asset you own such as a property or an inheritance through a trust fund etc.

If you happen to be self-employed, I'm sorry to say that financing is extremely tough.

Banks don't like lending to business people unless they've been in business for over five years and have a successful track record. If you're thinking of quitting your job and launching a startup, then hold on until your application has been approved. If you are self-employed, then you'll need a profitable track record going back at least five years.

The key is to show stability. This can be done through bank statements, income tax filings and audited financial statements. If you're a freelancer, you'll need to show contracts and tax filings along with bank statements going back a while to show that you have a steady stream of income.

Once all of this has been gathered, it's time to choose between a traditional mortgage or an FHA loan. I'll explain what an FHA loan is and how it compares to a traditional loan later in this chapter. Whichever choice you pick, the process is pretty much the same. It's just that the terms are different. So let's move onto the first stage of the process.

Pre-Approval

Most people skip this stage, but it will save you a ton of time and frustration. The pre approval stage is where you apply for a mortgage with the bank and they give you a letter stating how much you can get approved for and what your mortgage payment will be like.

This will help you figure out what kinds of properties you can look at. It also helps to present this letter to a seller since they'll know that there's a very good chance of the sale going through. During this process, the lending officer will calculate two metrics that determine how credit worthy you are.

The first metric is called the front ratio. This is calculated by dividing your mortgage payment by your monthly income (Turner,2016).

A good number is under 28%. For example if you earn $3,000 per month before taxes, a lender will feel safe if your mortgage payment is 28% of this number or lesser. This works out to $840 per month.

The second metric is the back ratio. This is calculated by dividing all of your debt payments every month by your monthly income (Greene, 2017). A good number is under 36%. If your car payments are $300, student loans debt payments are $300, and your mortgage payment is $840, your back ratio is 48%. This is a high number and most lenders will not consider you credit worthy. There are special circumstances when they'll approve your application.

If you have significant cash savings or an annuity that provides monthly income, they might let it slide.

However, most lenders will not approve such a high ratio.

Before applying for pre approval, calculate your own numbers to boost your chances. Either reduce your debt or increase your income to qualify. Having good numbers alone doesn't guarantee approval.

Theultimate decision is up to the lending officer. If they deem you too risky, they might offer you a poor interest rate.

Another important input into the decision is your Fair Isaac Credit Score or FICO score (Greene, 2017). Traditional lenders look for applicants who have scores greater than 675. This gets you in the door, but isn't a guarantee of approval. The higher your credit score is, the lower your interest rate will be. FHA lenders require a minimum score of 500 to qualify.

Locating Deals

Once you're pre pre-approved, you can begin searching for properties. There are certain properties that won't qualify for FHA financing and I'll explain this later in the chapter. Your properties generally cannot be in an advanced state of disrepair. A little sprucing up is fine, but don't target decrepit properties or anything that requires more than $6,000 worth of repairs.

This isn't a hard and fast limit. It's just an estimate since each bank is different. Once you've found a good deal and have negotiated a price, it's time to approach the bank and arrange financing.

Mortgage Application

This is the step where you'll be formally applying for a mortgage. If you've been pre-approved, the loan officer will make sure the conditions that existed at that stage are still valid. If they are, this process shouldn't take too much time. The most time consuming aspect is the inspection.

The bank will send a qualified home appraiser to determine the value of the property. This can be a tricky stage to navigate. There's nothing you have to do, but if you're investing in a property that needs some sprucing up, there is a chance that the appraiser could determine a value that is lesser than the sale price you've negotiated.

If the appraiser determines that the repairs needed are extensive the bank will refuse to finance the property. The same process applies with FHA loans as well. This is why it's best to stick to properties that are in need of small repairs but nothing too drastic. This way, you'll score a bargain and won't have to worry about the appraisal.

Once the appraisal is complete, the loan officer will present you with a formal offer for financing. This will contain the interest rate as well as the term of the loan. Your real estate agent will draw up a purchase agreement that will be sent to the seller for approval.

Once they approve, your agent will set up an escrow account.

You'll have to pay the down payment into this account and the bank will transfer the rest of the money into it. After a few days, the money is transferred to the seller and you'll need to pay closing costs. As mentioned previously, this amounts to three percent of the property's price. This pays the agent and all of the other professionals working behind the scenes to make your purchase work.

Once closing costs are paid, you will receive the title and will have to start making payments to the bank from the date listed in your contract with the bank. This concludes the financing process. If you've prepared and have gone through pre-approval, this step can be completed in as little as a few weeks.

The entire process from pre-approval to closing can take as long as six months. This includes searching for the property as well and negotiating with the seller so it's a reasonable time frame. You'll find that as you get better at locating deals, you'll be able to source, finance and close within three months or even less. It's best to take your time dotting the i's and crossing the t's on your first deal.

FHA Loans

FHA loans are backed by the government and this allows lenders to offer you more beneficial terms. For starters, the minimum credit score required is a lot less. Lenders will be happy with a score greater than 500.

Those who have scores greater than 580 can qualify to pay 3.5% down on their mortgage. Those who are below this threshold will have to pay 10% down.

Either way, the down payment requirements are far lower than the traditional 20% that banks require. This allows you to increase the leverage in your deal. Keep in mind that while the down payment might be low, the FHA doesn't give you lower monthly payments. The more you pay down, the lower your monthly payments will be.

Something to keep in mind with FHA loans is that the appraisal process is strict. The FHA does not finance rehabs of any kind and this means appraisers will sometimes disqualify properties that need repairs. You might find the same appraiser approves the property for a traditional loan but not for an FHA loan. The FHA has another program called the 203(k) which is reserved for rehab but it's subject to the condition in the paragraph below.

Another condition with the FHA is that the borrower needs to finance their primary residence. This means you need to live in the property. Therefore, turnkey rental investing is not possible with an FHA loan. You can, however, rehab and rent a property by using the 203(k) program.

The FHA does not like financing rehabbed homes with its money. This means any property that is up for sale within a year of its previous sale is not eligible for financing. Traditional lenders have no problem with this but the FHA doesn't consider such properties worthy. This means any property that has been rehabbed within the last three months is out.

Make sure you check with the seller about this since it will save you both a lot of time Typically, home flippers operate on three to six month timelines. You can either wait for the property to move out of the window to become eligible or you can find something else.

FHA loans allow you to make low down payments, but their overall costs might be higher. This is because you will have to pay private mortgage insurance or PMI for the entire duration of the loan. With traditional lenders, you'll need to pay PMI if you're paying less than 20% down. Once your equity crosses the 20% mark, the PMI payment is suspended. This is not the case with the FHA.

Make sure you run the numbers thoroughly when figuring out the income from a property. If the rental income subsidizes the entire payment including the PMI, there isn't anything to complain about.

However, it might be better for you to refinance the property down the road to reduce your monthly payment.

Hard Money Lenders

These are private lenders who fund real estate projects. A lot of them are former real estate investors who've moved to the money side of things and act as private banks for investors. They'll typically be able to spot the chances of failure or success pretty quickly and will tell you this in no uncertain terms.

Hard money lenders are best suited for rehabbers. Sometimes, a property is in too bad a shape to qualify for any kind of financing. Alternatively, you might not want to live in the property you're investing in. This means traditional banks and the FHA won't finance your purchase. Hard money lenders will be your only option.

The terms they offer can vary depending on your relationship with them and the type of deal you're looking to finance. They might ask you to pay 40% down or even be willing to finance a property with zero down. It depends entirely on how well you can negotiate. However, even the best negotiator won't be able to make a bad deal look good.

As explained earlier, hard money loans are usually employed as a bridge until the property becomes eligible for traditional financing. This allows the investor to earn their money back assuming the property appreciates.

The hard money lender doesn't expect you to borrow for more than a year and this is why their interest rates can be higher than usual. It isn't outlandish for them to charge you eight percent interest.

The risk with hard money lenders is that you might not be able to refinance and will be stuck with the property paying high interest rates.

For this reason, it's best for beginners to stay away from properties that require significant repair. Once you've gained experience, you can employ these tactics. You'll have assets to backup the risks you're taking and afford to take a chance or two.

Other Methods

If none of these options make sense to you then you'll have to come up with creative methods. One of the methods that most people use is to cut a wealthy relative or friend into the deal. You can create a partnership agreement that outlines both of your rights and earn a profit every month. Investors will usually require an exit so you'll need to account for this.

Another method that younger borrowers can employ is to ask their parents or relative to co-sign their mortgage application. This way. the bank knows that someone with more extensive credit is present on the application and their risk reduces. Both of these options have their pros and cons. You'll need to figure out what your personal relationships will look like if you decide to pursue these options.

There are some other ways you can finance your purchase. One of these is to draw on an existing line of credit such as equity in another property. Alternatively, you could ask the seller to finance your purchase. Some sellers might agree to this since it will result in them earning more money in the long run. However, most sellers of properties that need work are looking to sell quickly, so this won't always work.

Guaranteeing Approval

I must apologize for the clickbait. There is no way you can ever have a loan application guaranteed to be approved. However, you can significantly increase your chances by following a few simple steps. One of these steps is being prepared as you've already learned steps for. Most delays in the process are created by the applicant not getting the right paperwork back in time to the loan officer. Do this and you'll speed things up.

However, that doesn't help your approval chances. To understand how approval works you need to think like an underwriter. There are two individuals working at the bank who are instrumental in getting your loan approved. The first is the person you speak to face to face. This is the banker who is charged with bringing more loans to the bank.

These people earn a basic salary but are also paid a commission for every loan that is approved. They're just as invested in your approval as you are. Therefore, work with them. Some bankers can be frustrating to deal with and respond like automatons with a simple yes or no. The trick is to find a banker who understands that they stand to benefit from an approval as well.

Ask your real estate agent who their preferred banker is. Ask for a contact. This will get you started in the right direction. A helpful banker will point out the things you can do to increase your chances of approval. Get this person on your side and you'll make things easier.

The second person, who you'll never meet, is the underwriter. This is the person behind the scenes who's looking at the numbers. They deliberately never meet the applicants since they could become emotionally biased. The banker and underwriter will often not be present in the same branch either to avoid a bias. However, they will communicate and having the banker fight for your cause is helpful.

Even this doesn't guarantee approval, though. There are certain factors that underwriters look at. Make sure you're on the right side of these and your chances of approval will increase significantly. Ignore these and you'll be stuck in perennial apply and pray mode.

Property Type

Every lender has a preferred property type. If the lender you're applying to prefers commercial properties and you show up with a single family, it will be more difficult to change their mind should your application be denied. It's best to not waste your time applying.

A good banker (the person you talk to) will let you know of this beforehand.

Location and Condition

Each underwriter specializes in a particular location. These people know the neighborhoods inside and out and are very aware of the risks of loaning money in those neighborhoods. They've been carrying out location analysis on those properties since the day they were employed.

There are certain locations underwriters will never approve of and this becomes bank policy. Again, a good banker will let you know of this. Also enquire what kind of property conditions are they willing to put up with. Some lenders are okay with underwriting loans on properties that need fixing while some require them to be in pristine condition.

Loan Amount

You might think that lenders will only loan a certain maximum amount.

However, remember that banks earn money on interest. It's their job to loan as much money as possible. They want to loan a minimum amount, not a maximum. With banks, this is typically

$100,000. If you plan on making a large down payment, this might put your financing in jeopardy. Inquire as to what these minimums are before the pre-approval process.

LTV

LTV stands for loan to value. It's calculated by dividing the loan amount by the property value. If you borrow $80,000 from the bank to finance a $100,000 property, that's an LTV of 80%. While banks want to lend as much money as possible, this doesn't mean they're willing to expose themselves to undue risks.

For this reason, they like seeing some equity in the property they're financing. This is where the 20% down payment requirement comes from. In case you stop making payments and they need to foreclose, they'd like to recover some equity to cover their costs. Every lender has a ceiling on the LTV they're willing to accept so inquire about this.

Repayment

How will you plan on repaying the debt? Lenders want to see a source of repayment that will likely last for a long time. This means if you just landed a new job, they're not going to look at this as being particularly stable.

This is why I mentioned earlier that it's important to present as stable a picture as possible to the lender.

If you already have rental properties, they'll consider the income from those as well. However, no underwriter will ever consider 100% rentals. It's important to have some source of stable cash flow to present to a lender.

Experience

If you're applying for a large multifamily property, the lender will worry about your experience or lack of it. First time buyers are best off sticking to small multifarities or single family properties. Truth be told, this is done to protect the borrower as much as the lender.

Some people end up wanting to bite more than they can chew and this criterion protects them.

Do as much of the heavy lifting for your banker and you'll find that approval becomes easy. Remember that the underwriter is looking at multiple loan applications and not just yours. You make their job easier by providing extensive paperwork. Don't worry about submitting too much paperwork. The more proof you have, the more you ought to provide it.

If you do hear "no" from the lender, take it on the chin and move on. You can ask the customer facing banker why your loan was rejected and they might give you some pointers. You can try your luck at another lender or seek creative modes of financing at this point.

If you do get approved, congratulations! It's time to look at the strategies you can employ moving forward.

Chapter 7 Rental Investing Strategies

The great thing about real estate is that there aren't too many strategies that an investor can employ. This sounds strange because you'd think the more strategies that one can potentially employ, the more lucrative a field would be. However, this is not the

case. Look at the stock market for instance.

There is no end to the number of strategies you can employ to make money. You can go long term, short term, invest on the basis of macroeconomic factors, microeconomic factors, etc. How many people are actually successful investing stocks, though? The average person is more likely to fail than they are to succeed.

It's a bit like giving a hungry person all the food in the world. They want it, but it's probably not the best thing to do. They'll probably end up overeating and end up dissatisfied that they couldn't try everything that was put in front of them. Real estate doesn't offer too many different strategies.

What's more, every strategy has a lot of similar elements to it. You need to find a good bargain, finance it, and then either earn cash flow from it or sell it for a higher price.

That's really all it comes down to. The fancy terminology is just there to scare those away who don't want to do the work and that's a good thing.

When you want to earn money through rental investing, your aim is to increase your net worth over the long term and have your rentals pay you to own property. The rental income pays for maintenance and other expenditures and this allows you to control a lucrative asset for free. Everything that you do must be done with a view to ensure stability over the long term.

This is because you'll be assuming large amounts of leverage. Remember if your property doesn't provide you with cash flow, you need to make the mortgage payments out of pocket. Many investors don't consider this and end up creating debt holes for themselves

that they never emerge from. One of the reasons foreclosures are so prominent is because investors create cash burdens for themselves instead of aiming to own the asset for free (having it pay for itself.)

Keep this in mind when reading all of these strategies. None of them will work for you unless you execute the basics well. Prioritize stability and insist on the asset paying for itself. Any valid strategy will work once these are in place.

House Hacking

This is a great strategy for first time home buyers. It allows you to gain experience being a landlord and it puts a roof over your head all in one. The premise is simple. You locate a property that can be divided into multiple units. For example, let's say you find a single family home that has five bedrooms.

You can live out of one bedroom or the basement and place the other units for rent. You earn the income from your tenants and this allows you to pay for your mortgage and other expenses. Your living expenses are now zero since your asset is paying for itself. The best part is that since you'll be occupying the premises, you can qualify for an FHA loan.

This means your cash burden upfront will be low. However, keep in mind that if your cash burden is low, your monthly payment will be high. This reduces your chances of subsidizing your mortgage payment. Some people choose to accept a cash outflow since this is equivalent to paying rent.

For example, let's say your mortgage payment is $800 and you earn $600 as rental income. This means you need to pay $200 every month out of pocket to finance the purchase.

If you were paying this amount as rent before moving into your home, this might be an acceptable expense. It's going towards buying an asset after all.

Another option is to buy a small multifamily property. It's tougher to generate enough cash flow from these properties to subsidize your income. This is because each unit is separate and you cannot create a living space for yourself out of a nontraditional area like you

can do with a basement in a single family home. This means you will probably have a cash outflow.

As long as this is equal to or lesser than your regular monthly rental income and you can support it, it's a worthwhile purchase. Something else to remember when evaluating properties to house hack is that you need to apply the one percent rule to the overall rental income, not the income you will receive.

For example, if there are four units that generate $1,000 in rents every month and if the property is worth $100,000, this satisfies the one percent rule. If you occupy one of the units, your actual income is going to be less than $1,000. This is fine. As long as the overall potential income is greater than one percent of the property value, it's a good one to invest in.

The best house hacks, like every real estate investment, are those that require some work to be put into them.

Perhaps they need new cabinets or you could buy furniture and lease them as furnished apartments.

Cleaning the yard and improving landscaping can also justify increasing the rental price.

A particularly creative solution is to park a mobile home or build a tiny home in the yard and live in it. Place the other units for rent. This way, you can create a cash inflow from the property. House hacking places a huge amount of importance on the quality of your tenants and on how you manage your property.

It'll give you a great introduction to the various challenges of land lording and on the best ways of sourcing tenants. The good thing is you'll be on the property and can deal with any challenges immediately. If you have a full time job, it's a good idea to have a handyman on call who can take care of small issues.

Once you've lived in the property for a while and have built enough equity in it, you can refinance the property and draw a portion of the equity out. This gives you enough cash to put down on another property and you'll be able to expand your portfolio in this manner. Just remember that if you don't live in the property yourself, you won't qualify for an FHA loan.

Like with everything else, you need to be aware of the disadvantages. The primary disadvantage of house hacking is that you'll need to settle for less than optimal housing units if you want it to succeed.

After all, you're buying an entire property and living in a small portion of it. Not everyone will be happy with this.

You might also find yourself having to live in a neighborhood that is below the level of the one you can afford. If you can afford an A neighborhood, you might have to settle for a B neighborhood since you'll be able to buy multiple units there. The best way to deal with these short term discomforts is to remind yourself that you're building an asset.

In the long term, the benefits will completely outweigh the disadvantages. Some of these disadvantages include having to deal with tenants and maintenance issues at unearthly hours of the day. It's all good experience for you to learn from and you can apply these on your next investment.

Flipping Properties

Flipping homes is one of the most common real estate investment tactics. Since your objective is to earn rental income, you'll be holding onto the properties for a while before letting them go. The holding period is up to you. If the property is giving you a nice yield, you might as well hang onto it forever.

If you find dealing with the tenants painful then sell it and move on. Either way, the method of executing a successful flip remains the same. You source a property that needs fixing up at below market prices and offer accordion to the 70 percent rule mentioned previously.

The key to a successful flip is to estimate repairs correctly. You'll need to have good relationships built ahead of time to execute this.

The fact is that most experienced real estate investors are home flippers and this means time is of the essence. You'll need to quickly estimate how much the repairs will cost you and provide an offer that makes sense.

You'll also have to negotiate well since the seller isn't going to readily accept a price that is far below market value. While most properties that need rehab are REOs, this doesn't mean banks are going to do you any favors on the price.

This is why relationships are key. If you have an efficient real estate agent who can quickly send you the details along with relevant photos, you stand a better chance of assessing the damage and asking your contractor for informal estimates.

You should always budget a margin of safety into the repair costs before bidding.

This will prevent any nasty surprises. Something to remember is that the neighborhood type also matters.

If you're rehabbing something in a neighborhood that will attract less than desirable tenants, do you really want the headache of owning the property no matter the capital gains you'll realize with the ARV?

Remember that these properties won't qualify for FHA financing. You'll have to hold onto them for at least a year before you can successfully flip them.

If you manage to find someone who can finance it with a conventional mortgage, that's great, but if the property is in a low income area, then you're going to be targeting FHA buyers for the most part.

Many first time home flippers neglect to take the property's location into account and only look at the jump they'll realize in the property value.

You need to think like a rental property owner at the end of the day so always take the prospective tenants' quality and the neighborhood into account before making a decision.

Turnkey Rentals

Again, "turnkey" refers to properties that are ready to rent or are already generating cash flow for you. These kinds of properties don't offer the best bargains, but they offer the least number of headaches you'll have to deal with. If you want a passive source of income then these will suit you the best.

Having said that, you'll still need to deal with tenants and their issues unless you outsource this to a property management company. Most turnkey investors end up doing this because passivity is their aim. As long as they can collect the rental checks at the end of the month, they're happy owning the property.

The one percent rule is especially necessary here since you don't want to be addled with a property that is going to cost you a great deal of money. Finding turnkey rentals is pretty easy and you'll find that most real estate agents will have a bunch of them on hand. The banks also love these properties because they don't need any massive rehab costs and they're already generating cash flow.

This increases the likelihood that the borrower will be able to make payments.

Some of the best places to find turnkey rentals are on websites such as Zillow, LoopNet, and Roofstock.

These websites make it easy for you to analyze the property thanks to the wide variety of data they provide you with, such as crime statistics, schools, and recent sales.

They even grade the neighborhood for your convenience, but it's still best for you to tour the neighborhood yourself and take a look.

You'll be dealing with tenants who are already living in the place so you won't face any major issues from them. Some turnkey properties are offloaded by landlords who are sick of dealing with troublesome tenants. If you see a turnkey property selling for well below market price, this is probably the case. You can take a call as to whether you want to evict them or stay away from the deal.

Despite their ready cash flow nature, you need to budget for repairs down the road. Sometimes, the seller might be aware of a massive upcoming expense and will want to get rid of the property before this hits. You'll be stuck with the bill in this case. It helps to take a tour of the property before deciding to proceed.

What to Look for in a Property

No matter which strategy you choose to pursue, there are some things you need to look for in a rental property. Choosing the wrong property is something you want to avoid at all costs. You'll be stuck with a host of stressful issues and you'll probably end up losing money on the deal.

Here are a few tips to help you locate a good rental property.

Multiple Bedrooms

Unless you want a high turnover of tenants at your property, it's best to look for properties that have multiple bedrooms. Single family homes that have three or more bedrooms are the most stable rental investment there is. This makes sense because the average person who looks for such a home is probably newly married and has a child with another on the way.

When it comes to multifamily properties, it's best to stick to two bedrooms. These are quite common and make for stable rental properties. While not as stable as the single family home, you won't have to deal with your tenants moving out every few months as is often the case of single bedroom properties. Such tenants eventually start a family and need more space, which leaves you with a vacant property.

Invest in Younger Homes

The older a property is, the more you'll need to spend on maintaining it. What's more, these homes tend to be less energy efficient. You aren't liable to pay the utility bills, but your tenants will certainly know. This is especially the case if you're looking to attract high quality tenants. These people will not be okay with paying an additional $100 in heating bills every month in the winter. The quality of your carpet doesn't matter.

Having said that, older homes provide the best bargains. Be prepared to spend additional money on them since they tend to have a few skeletons in their closet. The trick is to balance the bargains that older homes provide with the quality of construction. The best way to learn is through experience. Stick to slightly older homes, somewhere in the five to ten year range before going all into homes that are older than 15-20 years.

Invest in Garages

This is closely tied to the bedroom question. A property that doesn't have a garage, especially a single family home, doesn't offer your tenants much incentive to stay put. In the case of multifamily properties, finding separate garages is a tough task. If the property has one, this is great. If not, then you'll just have to deal with higher turnover even if you've bought a multiple bedroom property.

In the case of single family homes, even if a property is available at a real bargain but doesn't have a garage, it might be best to pass on it with a view towards long term stability. Make it as easy as possible for your tenants to stay put. Once they start accumulating their junk in the garage, you'll know it'll be worth it because they're unlikely to move anytime soon.

Don't Pay for Utilities

Owners of older properties often advertise their rentals as having all utilities paid. The first thing that happens is that their tenants leave the air conditioning on all day long and leave the window open with the heat on in the winter. They won't inform the landlord about the dripping taps because they aren't paying for water.

Choosing to pay for utilities is a tricky thing. On one hand, you'll have no problems attracting tenants.

If they're high quality tenants, they'll be courteous. However, even the most courteous tenant is not going to care about your utilities bill.

If the math makes sense (it's hard to see how to be honest), then offer to pay for all utilities.

With single family homes, you'll need to take care of garbage collection and sewage as well. If you've structured your property to appeal to long term tenants, then you can pass these costs onto them. Multifamily homes typically won't come with all utilities paid. At the very least, you can have tenants pay for heat and electricity.

Some multifamily properties have a master meter system that monitors all utilities, except sewage, at once.

If this is the case, you can pass the water costs onto your tenants as well. Look for properties where the existing meter system can be converted to this. It's a great investment on your end.

Minimize Lawns

Note that I said minimize, not eliminate. If you're renting out a single family home, you need to have a decent lawn or outdoor family area. If everything else checks out, a long term tenant will maintain the lawn very well.

This is not the case with a multifamily home though.

In these cases, it's best to minimize the landscaping you need to do because you'll have to foot the bill. Your tenants won't be using the lawn or outdoor areas too much so it's best to stay away from properties that have huge lawns.

Parking and Location

You might have a great property but if parking is a headache, your tenants won't stay for long. Take a look at parking facilities. In the case of a multifamily home, how easy is it to find street parking? In crowded places, this is a real issue.

When it comes to single family homes, more is better. A good rule to follow is to have one less parking space than the number of bedrooms.

A three bedroom property needs to have two spaces for example.

Location matters quite a lot. You've already learned about this. Look at the entertainment options. The ideal property is close to entertainment but isn't in the thick of it. This keeps the noise levels down when necessary.

Smelly is Good

All of the previous points have highlighted the positives of a property. Now it's time to dive into the negatives. A savvy investor actively looks for problems in a property. This is what gives them a bargain after all.

A smelly property is something that most people run away from. However, that stink is what money smells like.

As long as there isn't an environmental issue or some sewage leak, a horrible smell can be easily dealt with. Replace the carpet, mop the floors with industrial standard bleach, clean the place to such an extent that your mother would be proud, and prime the floors and the walls/ceiling. Be careful when using oil based primers.

If you don't use a mask, you'll pass out and fall right into the primer which will take some explaining afterwards. Wash the walls with good soap. This helps get rid of any smoke residue.

The only exception is if the property has literally burned away. As a rule of thumb, replace the carpet no matter what. All of this should not cost you more than $2,000 if you choose to hire someone to do it. DIY this and your expenses will be even lower.

Smells can net you a bargain of over $5,000 or more on the asking price, so it's worth it.

The Potential Third Bedroom

In many neighborhoods the price difference between a two and a three bedroom property can be significant. Many two bedroom homes will have a hidden third bedroom in plain sight.

Check out spaces near the laundry room or try to partition one of the large bedrooms.

This will instantly boost the value of the property.

The average bedroom size is around 10X12 feet so look for potential bedrooms when you search for homes. This is especially true when you're looking to house hack. Create a third bedroom and you'll easily cover your mortgage, create a space for yourself, and build instant equity. Just make sure the cost of conversion is lower than the equity boost you'll receive.

Ugly Fixtures

Disgusting looking kitchen cabinets? Ugly light fixtures and door handles? Terrible looking bathroom fixtures? All of these might as well spell money as far as you're concerned.

The best thing is, all of these as easy wins for you. They boost your rental cash flow massively and they don't cost a lot. The same applies to paint and grimy driveways.

Mold

That's right! The M-word is an opportunity for you. Mold scares people away to a greater degree than anthrax does. The fact is that the deadly effects of mold are exaggerated (Turner, 2016).

Yes, it is harmful for people with certain immune system deficiencies, but getting rid of it is pretty simple.

It's all about ventilation. Make sure the vents are cleaned regularly and that the bathrooms have an exhaust fan and ventilation. Your mold issues will soon disappear. However, when most buyers hear the word, "mold," they run far away from it for fear of a lawsuit down the road. This means you can net a bargain.

The only exception is if there's mold in the basement. If this is the case, there's a water leak somewhere and you'll need to tear the whole thing apart. It's just not worth the hassle.

Leaky Roofs

A roof is a pretty essential thing. One that leaks is a liability. The costs of replacing a roof are pretty high. Right? Wrong! The average roof costs around $6,000 to replace (Schaub, 2016).

The trick is to shop around and ask as many contractors as possible. Ask the largest contractors and they'll stick you with a five figure bill. The smaller contractors will often do it for less.

You want to make sure to evaluate the efficiency of the contractor as well. However, take the time to shop around and don't dismiss a property just because its roof leaks. The equity boost will often outstrip the cost of the roof.

Junk and Jungles

This often happens in properties that have been lived in for a while. People hoard junk like there's no tomorrow and disposing of it is a real issue. The front yard also needs cleaning and all of this spells money to you. It's pretty easy to get rid of this stuff and give everything a good clean.

Stay Away From...

You want to look for problems to solve, but this doesn't mean you go around adopting every problem in sight. There are some that are far too much to deal with. The first is a bad neighborhood, or a neighborhood that doesn't fit your tenants' needs. You can't do anything to fix these issues so no matter how great a deal is, stay away from an ill-suited neighborhood.

The next is foundation issues. These are huge opportunities for a certain group of investors but if you're starting out, stay away from these. It'll cost too much to fix and there's no guarantee the problem will be solved.

Lastly, stay away from shared driveways or shared anything. This puts the value of your property in the hands of the person next door. If they happen to be unclean or start hoarding things in the common area, no tenant will want to live next to them. There's nothing you can do about it either because it's their property after all.

Chapter 8 Smart Management

Even toasters are "smart" these days so why can't you be a smart landlord? Many investors shoot themselves in the foot because

they don't take good enough care of their properties. I'm not talking about letting the place rot or allowing pests to roam free. They unknowingly end up attracting the wrong kind of tenants and drive their investment into a hole.

Managing your rentals can seem to be a full time job, but there's no reason it needs to take the majority of your day. The first decision you'll need to make is whether you want to be a DIY landlord or hire a management company.

Management Companies

Once you buy a property your agent will likely introduce you to a few property management companies. These companies look after every detail of your property and charge you a fee for it. Many investors prefer such arrangements since it makes their purchase almost passive. However, it needs to make sense financially as well.

Here are the things that most property management firms handle:

1.　　Rent collection

2.　　Tenant sourcing

3.　　Maintenance

4.　　Landscaping

5.　　Evictions

6.　　Anything else you can think of

In return for these services, they will charge you a portion of the rent which is usually 10%. If your tenant pays you $1,000 per month, the firm will charge you $100. This doesn't sound like much. However, most firms charge a one time fee when replacing tenants. This can be as much as 100% of the rent. They might even charge you a renewal fee every year even if the tenants stay put.

This impacts your bottom line massively. There's something else to consider. How can a company make profits by earning just 10% of monthly rentals?

The answer is volume. Your property isn't the only one they're managing. A successful management company usually has at least 100 properties on their portfolio.

This allows them to pay their staff and office bills. They also have special relationships with contractors in the area and provide quick maintenance services.

However, they'll charge a higher fee when working with their preferred contractors. Most landlords don't pay attention to this and end up paying thousands for something that ought to cost a few hundreds.

At the end of the day, no one is going to care for your property more than you. It's your money after all. You might be a terrible landlord at first, but you'll eventually learn and get better. The management company might be decent but they have little to no incentive to prioritize your property over others.

Imagine a prospective tenant inquiring about your place. If they seem to be good tenants, you'll likely rush over and show them the place. The management company has no incentive to do this. As far as they're concerned, one tenant is the same as another. They could rent any one of the 100 properties on the firm's roster and the company still gets paid.

The flip side is that you don't need to worry about dealing with phone calls and issues at ridiculous times of the day. Your time will be freed up and you can spend it on things that truly matter to you. It's up to you to decide whether the cost of a lower yield is worth freeing up your time.

When screening firms, it's best to adopt a guilty before innocent approach. Assume all of them are bad and ask them to prove they're good.

This way, you'll adopt a more realistic approach. I'm not saying all firms are bad. It's just that you might get carried away with the marketing promises of such companies and not pay attention to the details.

The DIY Landlord

Landlording is tough and it's best for you to gain experience as quickly as possible. If you truly hate the experience then you'll have more justification to hire a property management firm. Your aim throughout the process should be source tenants who will stay for as long as possible and those that will give you the least number of headaches.

Your first step should be to prepare the property for leasing. Make sure the place is clean and that everything looks as good as it should. If your property is furnished make sure the furniture is clean and looks good. Your tenants will most probably be swinging by after work so make sure the lights work and that the faucets aren't dripping.

Advertising

You need to let people know you have a great property to rent. Make sure to take good photos.

It might be worthwhile to hire a local photographer who can showcase your property in the best light. This is something Airbnb owners do quite a lot and it helps attract high quality tenants.

Place ads on Craigslist, in your yard, and in the local classifieds. You can also list your property for rent on the MLS and have agents bring tenants to you. You'll have to pay a fee but it might be worth the cost. The agent will have experience dealing with people and will be able to screen potential tenants. Let everyone in your network know that you're looking for a tenant. This is the best form of marketing since the person will be vouched for.

Screening

Prior to placing ads, get yourself a Google Voice number. This number can be redirected to your own phone and down the road you can redirect this to a contractor or to a maintenance person in case you happen to be unavailable. It's free so you might as well use it. Once you start accepting phone calls, make sure you pre-screen your tenants.

Here are the best screening criteria that will ensure you land high quality tenants all the time:

1.   Their pretax income must be at least thrice the rent you're charging

2.   Their credit score must be at least 620

3.   They must have proof of income and must be able to furnish it upon request

4.   They must have references from prior landlords

5.   No more than two people can occupy a bedroom

You can add another criterion regarding smoking on the premises. They could smoke outside but not inside the property. Some landlords prefer non-smokers, so it's your choice. Explain these provisions to your prospective tenant on the phone instead of interrogating them about it. Stick to these criteria solely and explain that if they don't meet these criteria during the application process, they likely won't be able to lease your property.

Do not ask them anything about race, skin color, sex, religion, disability, national origin or familial status. You cannot even use these words without sounding discriminatory, so stay away from these topics at all costs.

Application

Schedule all of your viewings in a 30 minute or hourly window so you don't need to travel to and from the property constantly.

Having multiple people view the property is a good way to generate some competition for it. You'll attract motivated applicants. If they're interested in leasing your property, have them fill out an application form.

The form might seem like overkill, but it's a great way to screen tenants. High quality tenants will have no issues filling out information formally. They'll have adequate proofs that you need. Your form should collect the following information at a minimum:

1. Names

2. Date of births

3. Social security numbers

4. Contact numbers

5. Emergency contact number

6. Addresses over the past five years

7. Contact information of previous landlords

8. Resumes with links to LinkedIn profiles

9. Contact information of their employers/managers

10. Signatures

Collect an application fee once they're done filling this out. The point isn't to make money, it's to screen tenants who are motivated. You can collect a small fee of $30. This will cover your costs to run a background check. Also make sure you have a standard release of information statement on your application.

Use the criteria mentioned before to screen your tenants.

Call all of their references as well as their employer to verify their worthiness as a tenant. Ask the previous landlord if the tenant received their security deposit back and whether they would rent to these tenants again. Once you've conducted this process, it's time to let your tenants know whether they've been accepted or rejected.

When rejecting a tenant, it's best to let them know in writing. Send them a letter by mail and keep a copy for yourself. Clearly outline why you're rejecting them. Make sure you're not being discriminatory when rejecting them. Process all applications on a first come first served basis to avoid any such allegations. Make sure you keep your emotional biases in check as well.

If you wish to inform a tenant they've been accepted, let them know by phone. However, make sure you collect a holding deposit from them that's payable within 24 hours if they're not moving in within that time period.

This is to ensure they don't skip out on you and find some other place to rent. You can even collect this deposit when having them apply. You'll have to return this money to the applicants you'll reject.

You can lump the holding deposit with the security deposit which should be equal to at least two months' rent. Have them sign an agreement that if they don't move into the property within a certain date, their deposit will be forfeited and they'll need to apply again.

Download a state specific rental agreement from ezlandlordforms.com and have them sign it. Make sure you offer

your tenant multiple ways to pay rent. This can be through online services such as PayPal or through other services such as Dwolla or Venmo.

Moving in

You're almost there! Before your tenant moves in, create a move in condition report. Take photographs of the property as well as any damages. Have the tenants submit any pictures they might think appropriate and document everything. Sign the report and provide them with a copy. Once this is done, accept the first month's rent and hand over the keys.

All you need to do now is take care of maintenance, bookkeeping and taxes! Don't let this get you down though. You're now officially a landlord.

Maintenance

Maintenance might seem like a huge task but there are some common areas that always pose problems. Deal with these and everything else will fall into line.

Appliances not Working

Electronic items have a tendency to break down right when you need them the most. Have someone on hand to quickly repair them since they annoy tenants the most. No one wants to see laundry pile up because the washing machine hasn't been fixed for a week. When the time comes to replace them, buy used. Avoid fancy stove tops that look great but are tough to repair.

Water Leaks

Water leaks will usually spring near the windows and in the roof. When your tenant reports it to you, get it handled as quickly as possible. If not dealt with on time, the wood will rot and you'll have a much bigger problem to deal with. Hire the best contractor to get this fixed and don't worry about spending more than needed.

Another area of water leaks is under the sink. This can be fixed much more easily than a leak in the structure on the building.

More often than not it's because of ill-fitting pipes. Hire a plumber to make this go away. Then, there are the slow drips from faucets. Leaking toilets can also add to your utility bills over time. Get these fixed quickly. If you need to replace the faucet then buy a good quality one. Don't buy plastic faucets that need to be replaced every year.

Hot Water Running Out

If the hot water runs out, it's likely a problem with the heater. Check to see whether the heater itself is damaged or the coil within it is. Replacing the entire heater will cost you upwards of $500, but the coil or element inside it can be replaced for as little as $20.

Pests

This is a big one. Roaches, rodents and other bugs love troubling landlords at odd hours of the night. The most frustrating aspect of this is they occur because the tenants aren't clean. It's a good idea to include a clause in your lease where pest control becomes the tenant's responsibility after a month of living in the property. This way, you can be certain it isn't your fault.

This approach doesn't work for multifamily properties since it can be impossible to tell where the bugs are coming from. Be proactive and eliminate all problems as quickly as possible. Have a pest control service on speed dial and deal with it quickly before it turns worse.

Garbage Disposal Issues

It's best to remove these entirely since they break down all the time. More often than not, it's because there's something in there that shouldn't, such as bones or forks. Sometimes, the gears in there get stuck and you might need just a wrench to fix it. If the motor is spoiled then it will cost you a few hundred bucks to fix it.

Clogged Pipes

These can either be a tenant's or a landlord's responsibility. If the toilet is clogged and nothing else is, it's the tenant's responsibility to get it cleared. Call a plumber and bill the tenant for the service. If all pipes seem to be clogged, then it might be your responsibility since there might be something wrong with the internal piping in the property.

Furnaces

These often happen in fall when your tenant will start using the furnace after a long break. It's worth carrying out a routine inspection before the weather gets cold to make sure everything works. The most common issue is a pilot light going out. This is easy to fix. However, if there's a gas leak you might have a larger problem on your hands.

These don't cover the entire world of issues you'll face of course. However, carry out annual preventive maintenance on all of these items and you'll ensure your problems won't overwhelm you. Here are the things you need to carry out at such times:

1. Change furnace filters

2. Remove dust from fridge coils

3. Replace smoke detector batteries

4. Flush the heater

5. Make sure CO detector is working

6. Clean sediment from shower heads

7. Check expiration dates on fire extinguisher

8. Clean gutters

9. Check the pump in the sump

10. Caulk any doors and windows as needed

11. Fertilize the lawn

12. Check water valves

13. Clean and paint the exterior

14. Make sure faucets and bathrooms don't have mold in it

15. Test garage door openers

16. Inspect for termite or bug infestation

17. Tighten all handles and screws wherever applicable

You and Your Tenant

Most landlords don't realize that their tenants will behave exactly as the landlord expects them to behave. Allow your tenant to leave your property dirty and they'll continue to do so. Let late rental payments slide repeatedly and you can expect them to always pay late. Allow them to move people into your property without notice and you'll find them taking advantage of this repeatedly.

You need to maintain a business-like atmosphere between you and your tenant. This doesn't mean you need to be harsh. Don't confuse friendliness for being friends. Draw a firm line and let them know when they cross it. The most common issue is late rental payments.

Charge them a hefty late fee and if they repeatedly pay you late or ask for extensions, let them know that they need to move out. It might even be worth paying them to move out since evictions will cost you money. A standard eviction will cost you $5,000 or more so you want to avoid this as much as possible.

Another area of conflict, particularly in multifamily properties, will be between your tenants. One person might not appreciate the noise another makes and so on. The best thing to do is to examine whether the offending behavior is against the terms of the lease. If so, don't waste any time notifying the tenant that their behavior is unacceptable. If they repeat the behavior, let them know they have to leave.

If it's an issue that isn't in the lease, let the matter rest for a couple days. More often than not, the tenants will sort it out amongst themselves. Always let your tenants' phone calls go to voicemail and then check the message they leave you. You'll open yourself up to a lot of drama otherwise.

Another common instance of bad behavior is moving in unapproved tenants or pets. Let them know that everyone who moves into your property needs prior approval. Everyone needs to apply and pay the application fee before moving in. This way you'll always know who's living in your property. Your primary tenant might be wonderful but their partner might be a dodgy character. Don't expose yourself to such liability.

Pets are a tough question. On one hand, you can charge higher rent and they improve your tenants' quality of life. However, they tend to create dirt and this makes cleaning up a headache. Here's a simple rule of thumb. If the property is nice, allow pets. If it isn't, don't. The logic is that nice properties attract clean people and they'll be more likely to be responsible pet owners.

Multifamily properties should not have pets for the same reason. The tenants here will be more transient and you don't want to expose yourself to huge clean up costs.

If you find that your property is making you feel harassed or you aren't able to enjoy the benefits of ownership, your system needs fixing. You've probably allowed things to become too casual and aren't enforcing strict rules.

Conclusion

Everyone wants to earn that sweet, passive rental income but not many are willing to face up to how much work rental properties take.

Are you willing to put in the work that is necessary to make this a success? Hopefully you now understand why maintaining a great mindset is essential.

Without a business mindset, your rentals are going to run your life. You want it to be the other way around.

If you think that adopting a business mindset means you need to be cold or hard hearted then you've misunderstood what this means.

Being business like means you value your time and property above all else.

Your tenants are not the ones taking the risks by investing in your property.

It's your money in there. They don't care about your money or how much hard work you've put into making it agreeable to live in.

It's your job to stand up for your efforts and rights. Don't assume your tenants will automatically appreciate all the work you've put in.

That's not their job.

You're the one who's ultimately responsible for the way your properties are run.

There's no one else out there who can fix things for you. Recognize that this is a good thing and take action accordingly.

Remember to return to the basics and educate yourself with regards to how successful rentals work.

Pick the right strategies and your wealth will grow exponentially.

Rental property investing is a fantastic way to grow your net worth.

You simply need to play the game according to the rules. Everything else will take care of itself.

Let me know how this book has helped you by leaving me a review.

I wish you all the luck in the world. Happy rental investing!

References

Dweck, C. S. (2016). Mindset : the new psychology of success. Ballantine Books.

Greene, D. (2017). Long-distance real estate investing : how to buy, rehab, and manage out-of-state rental properties. Biggerpockets Publishing.

Schaub, J. W. (2016). Building wealth one house at a time, updated and expanded, second edition. Mcgraw-Hill Education - Europe.

Turner, B. (2016). The book on rental property investing : how to create wealth and passive income through smart buy & hold real estate investing. Bigger Pockets Publishing, Cop.

Image References

apartment. (2020). In pixabay. apartment-view-. (2020). In pixabay. architecture. (2020). In pixabay. architecture-building. (2020). In pixabay. condominium. (2020). In pixabay. facade. (2020). In pixabay.

finance. (2020). In pixabay. house. (2020a). In pixabay. house. (2020b). In pixabay.

house-architecture-city-. (2020). In pixabay. house-keys-. (2020). In pixabay.

house-real-estate. (2020). In pixabay. houses. (2020). In pixabay.

interior. (2020). In pixabay. kitchen. (2020). In pixabay. living. (2020). In pixabay.

luxury. (2020). In pixabay. property. (2020). In pixabay. purchase. (2020). In pixabay. skyscraper. (2020). In pixabay.